DESIGNS FOR CHILDREN

FURNITURE, ACCESSORIES & TOYS

AGATA TOROMANOFF

DESIGNS FOR CHILDREN

FURNITURE, ACCESSORIES & TOYS

CONTENTS

INTRODUCTION

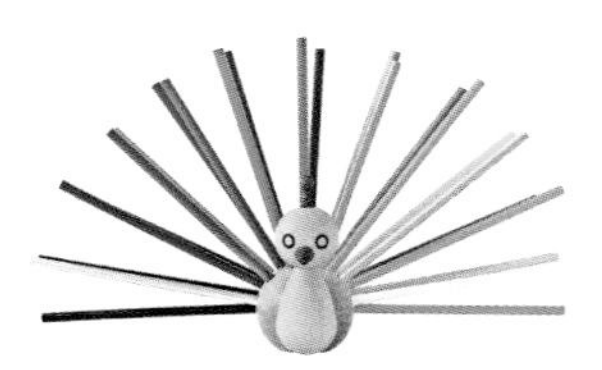

Decorating and furnishing a child's room is a very pleasant task, but it is not always as easy as it seems. Making the right choice from a wide range of furniture and accessories and imagining your children's needs as they grow are two essential criteria for finding the right furniture. But it's also important to make sure that the furniture fits the configuration of the room and stimulates creativity without hindering movement. It is in their room that children will live and dream, imagine the world and their future. They need to feel happy and protected there. A child's room should not only be functional, it should also have a playful aspect, create a friendly atmosphere, and reflect, through its shapes and colors, the joy of living and the unbridled energy characteristic of children.

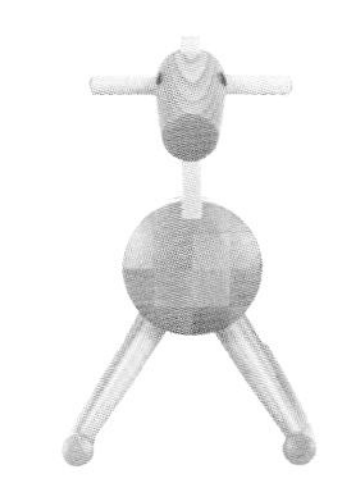

Designing the interior of a child's room is a creative process that requires some imagination and originality, while asking yourself certain questions such as: What are the ideal dimensions of a table for drawing and playing? What type of seat will work best for my child? How do I choose shelves to place dolls, books, and toys in the right order so that they are accessible to little hands? And where will bulky items be stored? Just for the seat, you will have to choose between a very comfortable model like a beanbag, a more classic wooden chair, a stacking stool, or a child's chair with or without armrests. Since children often play on the floor, you should think about providing a soft and safe surface. Another important point is safety: light furniture tends to tip over, so this is an aspect to consider when making your choices. What decorative patterns and colors will appeal to your child? And finally, what are the best materials, which are the most sustainable and practical to maintain?

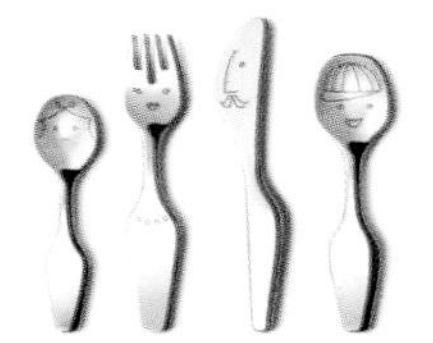

This book presents a wide selection of furniture, accessories, and design toys that offer simple answers to these questions. They can be combined or used individually depending on the space available and the atmosphere you wish to create, but they must also harmonize with your child's personality. It is essential to find a good balance between decoration, practical solutions (storage areas), and playfulness. The ideas we describe are original, inventive, and stimulating. Creating furniture and accessories for children is a challenge to which designers have responded by creating amazing projects. More and more internationally renowned designers are interested in furniture for the little ones and have been creating exceptional objects, on the border between functionality and play. So let's give children the opportunity to have fun in their own little kingdom.

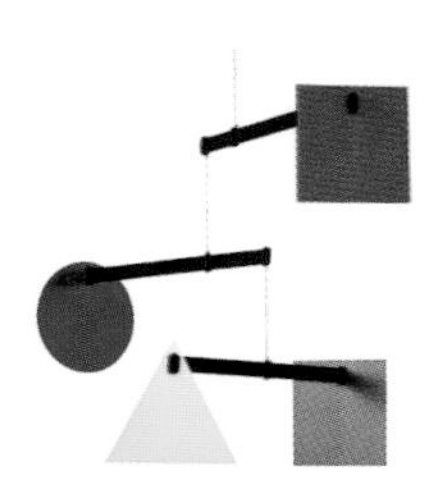

All over the world, design-conscious parents want to pass on their passion for beautiful pieces of furniture to the younger generation. Others simply want to choose children's furniture that has been universally recognized for its practical and aesthetic qualities. Here everyone will find design masterpieces adapted to the size and shape of children, as well as furniture specially designed for them. Some of the models are timeless and will never go out of fashion, while others are recent creations using the latest technological developments. We hope that parents will share the pages of this book with their children and introduce them to the fabulous world of design. They will learn to play with shapes, space limitations, materials, and colors. Enjoy!

NOTES.

FURNITURE

#(ARM)CHAIRS

Although children love playing on the floor and can be bundles of energy in constant motion, there are still many activities that are better performed while sitting quietly in a chair. Reading books, drawing at a table full of crayons, or making cut-outs from colorful paper may be among them. To enjoy creative activities that require some concentration, one needs an elegant and comfortable chair, best of all a scaled-down version of an iconic design for adults.

BARCELONA® CHAIR, CHILD'S MODEL, LUDWIG MIES VAN DER ROHE, CA. 1929 KNOLL, INC.

Timelessly elegant, comfortable in shape, and combined with a footstool for resting the legs, the Barcelona® Chair is a stylish element for any child's room. Mies van der Rohe envisioned it for the German Pavilion at the 1929 International Exposition in Barcelona. Thinking at the time of a possible visit from the King and Queen of Spain, the designer came up with a grand and graceful shape. Scaled down, it does indeed feel like a throne for little royals.

637 BABY UTRECHT ARMCHAIR, GERRIT THOMAS RIETVELD, 1935/2015 (CHILD'S MODEL) CASSINA COLLEZIONE I MAESTRI

What is revolutionary about the Utrecht Armchair by Dutch architect and designer Gerrit Thomas Rietveld is its curious structure. The slanted seat with its high back rests nonchalantly on the floor, as if the armchair were suspended only by the two massive armrests. The firm, poplar plywood frame is covered with foam and polyester padding for maximum softness, which creates an interesting visual contrast with its geometric shape (Rietveld's other iconic seats are known for their hard shells). The most playful version has zig-zag top-stitching visible against vividly colored upholstery.

WOMB CHAIR, CHILD'S MODEL, EERO SAARINEN, 1948 KNOLL INC.

To create this inviting chair, Eero Saarinen and Florence Knoll teamed up with a boat builder who worked with fiberglass. By pushing the borders of that era's techniques and materials, they designed a novel and extremely comfortable seat. While Knoll's brief read: *"I want a chair that is like a basket full of pillows...something I can curl up in,"* Saarinen focused on creating a shape that would encourage relaxation. Standing on a metallic base, the soft shell embraces the sitter.

BERTOIA CHILD'S DIAMOND™ CHAIR, HARRY BERTOIA, 1952/1955 (CHILD'S MODEL) KNOLL, INC.

Italian American furniture and jewelry designer Harry Bertoia was also a sculptor, which explains his bold approach to selecting materials – both the use of welded wire and the unusual form. Mastering the study of body dynamics, Bertoia envisioned a volume that is sensual and organic as well as ergonomic. The wire grid of the Diamond Chair is well suited to the human shape despite the material's sturdiness. The industrial metal gains aesthetic value in this sculptural form. The seat has been in continuous production since 1953 (the child's model followed two years later). It is a great addition to any playroom.

UP5 ARMCHAIR, CHILD'S MODEL,
GAETANO PESCE, 1969
B&B ITALIA

The portfolio of the Italian designer Gaetano Pesce includes many amazing chairs but UP5 from 1969 is probably the most inventive one. Made of polyurethane foam, a highly innovative material at that time, the seat has a very sensual and amusing shape inspired by the female body. Its soft and snuggly form beckons the sitter, while its rounded edges are perfectly safe for even the most energetic little climbers. A spherical leg-rest, which can be also used as a pouf, adds to the armchair's originality.

366 JUNIOR ROCKING CHAIR, JÓZEF CHIEROWSKI, 1962/2015 (CHILD'S MODEL) 366 CONCEPT

The 366 Armchair is an iconic Polish design envisioned by Józef Chierowski in the 1960s. Its perfect proportions make it a modest yet stylish classic. The base is made of ash wood that has been seasoned for at least 7 years before being used in production. It has wide armrests and carries an upholstered shell. The Junior Rocking Chair, just like the original model, is a recent reinterpretation by the team of 366 Concept, a Polish brand which has resumed the production of the armchair.

TICKING CLOCK ROCKING CHAIR KID, THOMAS DARIEL MAISON DADA

Ticking Clock Kid is made of solid beech wood with a matte painted finish. To complement the comfort provided by gentle rocking, the seat is upholstered. In addition, the traditional shape of an armchair gets a contemporary touch with its gigantic circular side (the adult and child's models are identical). Visually dominating the structure, the wheels add another dimension to the rocking. The scaled-down model is available in two lovely colors – sky blue and dusty pink.

CHAIR N65, CHILD'S MODEL,
ALVAR AALTO, 1935
ARTEK

Called a *smaller sibling* of Chair 65 by Alvar Aalto, this iconic design from 1935 was a perfect candidate for down-sizing. The round seat (characteristic of Aalto's designs), L-shaped legs and sightly curved backrest provide maximum comfort for children. With a seat height of 15 inches (38 cm.), it works well with low tables and for small children. The chair's timeless shape, as well as its light color, matches all kinds of interiors. The clean lines and natural feel of the birch wood express the spirit of Scandinavian design.

BEAR AND RABBIT PLAY CHAIRS, PLAY COLLECTION ŒUF NYC

A simple plywood chair doesn't have to be boring. Brooklyn-based and family-run studio Œuf has proven this by adding bear or rabbit ears to a classical shell. This original variation can be enhanced with a collection of funny stickers of faces that can be added to the backrest. Made of Baltic birch plywood, the series, like all the brand's furniture, is produced in an environmentally friendly and certified facility in Latvia. With a seat suited to children ages two to six, the chairs match the Œuf play table in the same collection.

SERIES 7™ CHAIR, ARNE JACOBSEN, 1955/2005 (CHILD'S MODEL) FRITZ HANSEN

The iconic Series 7™ chair by Danish master of design Arne Jacobsen demonstrates his excellent wood lamination technique. The chair was relaunched for children in 2005. The minimalist structure of the shell, sitting on a 4-legged base, is simple but elegant, and works in any type of space. As it is stackable, the design is also highly practical. Available in a range of sophisticated hues, it also comes with powder-coated legs in a matching color for those who want a monochromatic look.

PANTON JUNIOR CHAIR, VERNER PANTON, 1959/1960 VITRA

The children's version of this icon of modern design is approximately one quarter smaller than the full-size Panton Chair. Designed by Verner Panton, it is an all-plastic chair with a glossy lacquer finish. Its dynamic and ergonomic shape is perfect for small, restless children. It is also imaginative and appealingly offbeat. One can feel oddly suspended above the ground in this timeless chair. Created from a single piece of plastic, it is also easy to maintain.

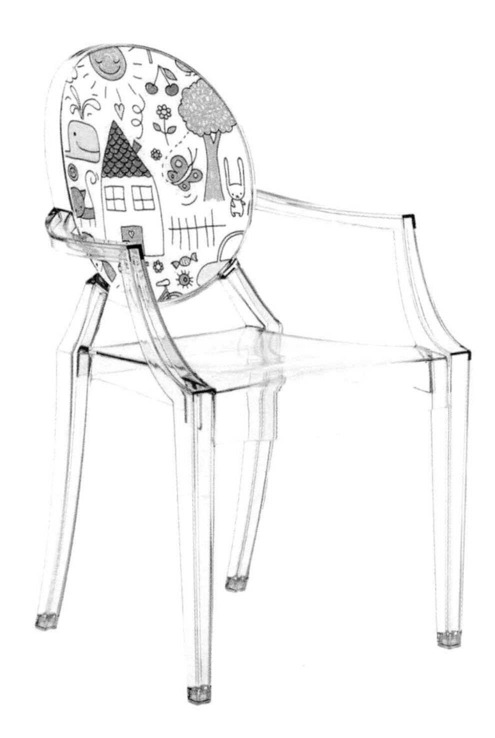

LOU LOU GHOST ARMCHAIR, PHILIPPE STARCK, 2008 KARTELL

At the beginning there was the Louis Ghost, Philippe Starck's bold reinterpretation of the baroque Louis XV armchair. Described by the manufacturer as "the world's bravest example of the injection of polycarbonate in a single mold," it is durable while giving the impression of being fragile. Just like the prototype, the identical scaled-down model called Lou Lou Ghost is also stackable. The throne-like chair can be made even more playful as it also comes in pink or light blue in addition to the transparent crystal version. It can be customized with a colorful drawing on the backrest.

ALMA CHAIR, JAVIER MARISCAL, 2006 MAGIS ME TOO

As children like using chairs with inventive shapes, designers are keen on experimenting with forms, materials, and colors. Javier Mariscal's Alma Chair comes in four hues, which represent the seasons: green for spring, orange for summer, brown for autumn and white for winter. The designer also put great effort into decorating the backrest of the chair with raised floral and animal patterns.

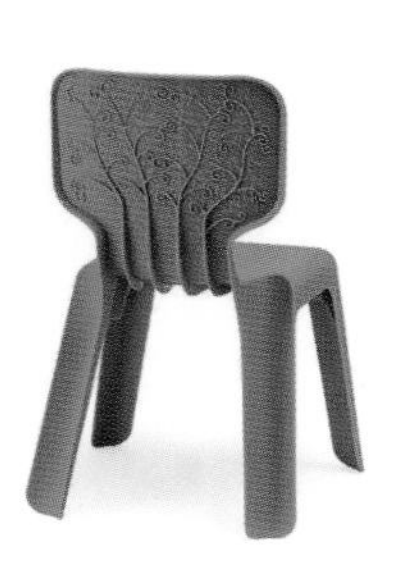

SEGGIOLINA POP CHAIR,
ENZO MARI, 2004
MAGIS ME TOO

Enzo Mari invented a very light yet strong construction for Seggiolina Pop (2004). The chair weighs less than one kilogram (35 oz.), allowing children to move it around easily without the help of adults. Its unpretentious and fun shape makes it look as if it were inflated. It is also easy to climb on and comfortable to sit in.

LITTLE NOBODY CHAIR, KOMPLOT DESIGN HAY

Copenhagen-based studio Komplot Design first designed a mono-block dining chair that used only textiles in its structure (a material that is one hundred percent recyclable plastic converted into felt). Molded in a single piece, the chair resembles a stone more than a seat. The kids' version of this ingenious shape was simply a must. No hard edges to cause harm and a soft finish to prevent scratching the floor (or making noise) are only some of the designer's solutions that make it a perfect piece of furniture for a child's room.

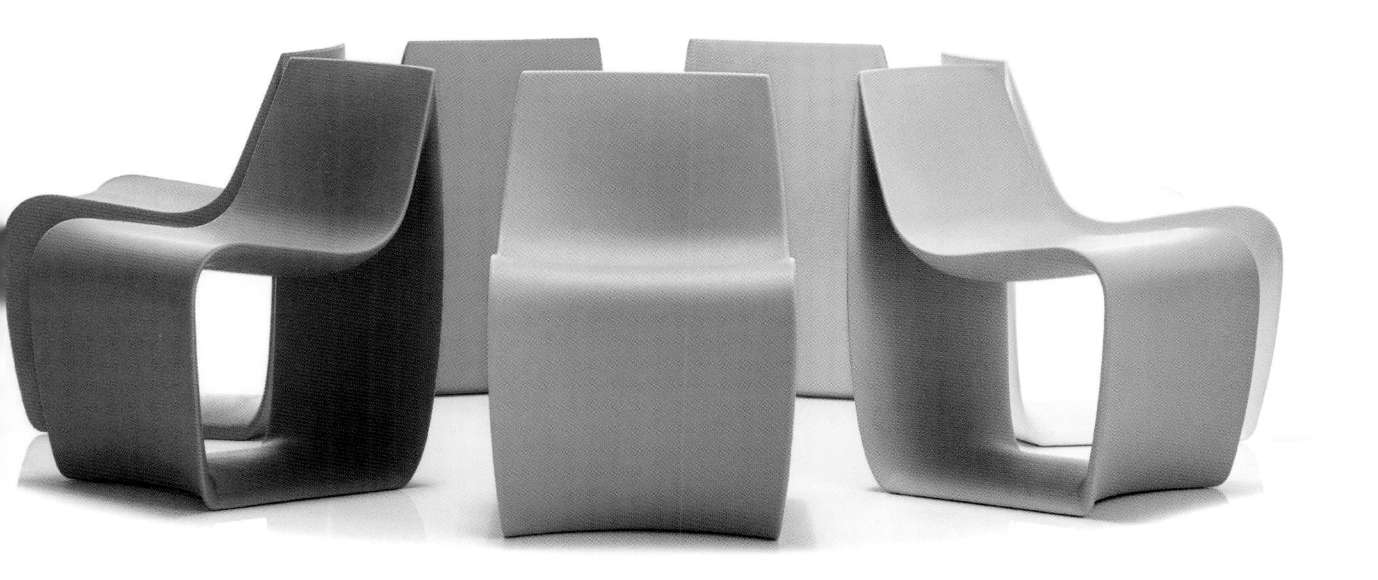

SIGN BABY CHAIR,
PIERGIORGIO CAZZANIGA, 2017
MDF ITALIA

The monolithic Sign Baby chair was created to celebrate the tenth anniversary of MDF Italia's iconic eponymous chair for adults. The version dedicated to the young generation is one third smaller than the original, and is meant for children between 3 and 10. Manufactured from polyethylene in a palette of seven vivid colors, it uses rotational molding technology. The dynamic silhouette creates a shape that is adjusted to the body's shape, and there is even space for storage below the seat. Resilient as well as easy to maintain, the Sign Baby chair can also be used outdoors.

TRIOLI ARMCHAIR, EERO AARNIO, 2005 MAGIS ME TOO

Designed by leading contemporary Scandinavian designer, Eero Aarnio, Trioli is a simple yet inventive piece of furniture. A curved backrest is at the heart of the design, with a spacious shelf that offers two heights depending on which way up the chair stands (each creates a cozy seating area). Turned onto its front, Trioli quickly transforms into a rocking horse. Supporting all three options is a rounded handle on the back that makes turning the chair quite easy and provides something to hold onto when in rocking-horse mode. Trioli can be used both indoors and outdoors.

LITTLE BIG CHAIR, BIG-GAME STUDIO, 2017 MAGIS ME TOO

The trio of Big-Game studio – Augustin Scott de Martinville, Elric Petit, and Grégoire Jeanmonod – envisioned a piece of furniture that would grow with the child. A simple system makes it possible to adjust the seat to three different levels; the chair can be used by kids ages 2 to 6. Standing firmly on the ground thanks to its flat legs, with its playful mix of a wooden base and plastic shell the chair almost resembles an organic creature. Produced in red, white, and blue, the colors enhance the dynamic shape of the chair.

JULIAN CHAIR, JAVIER MARISCAL, 2005 MAGIS ME TOO

Chairs for children do not necessarily have to mimic those for adults. Some inventive designs are witty forms inspired by animals. The Julian, invented by Javier Mariscal for Magis, is a chair that resembles the silhouette of a cat. The pet's paws become the chair's legs and its face, complete with whiskers, forms a comfortable backrest. Executed in bright colors, it is a fun chair and as it's made of polyethylene, it can easily be used outdoors.

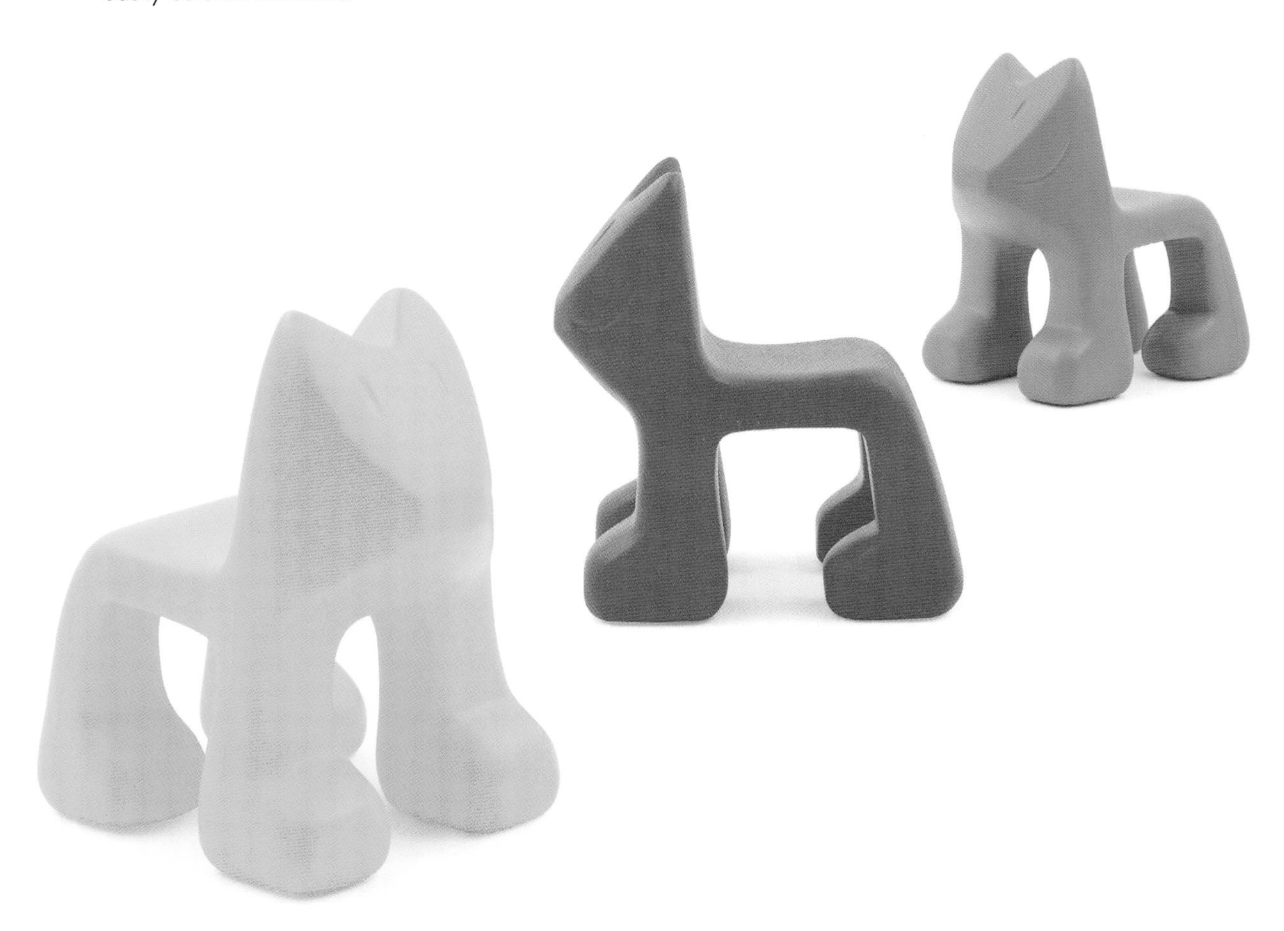

MARRY
ME
SMILE
JOY
PRIVÉE

MOUETTE ARMCHAIR, TOLIX®, 1927/1935 (CHILD'S MODEL)

The French designer Xavier Pauchard originally designed this armchair for his own children in the 1920s. Envisioned as a miniature version of his famous C Armchair, an iconic piece of furnishing for the luxurious ocean liner "Le Normandie," it is characterized by its graceful tubular back and armrests. Made of steel, both armchairs were a triumph for the designer's innovative experiments in working with metal. The techniques he introduced allowed him to achieve any shape he envisioned. Sturdy and practical, the chair is also timelessly elegant. Manufactured by Tolix®, the brand founded by Pauchard, it can be personalized with the child's first name.

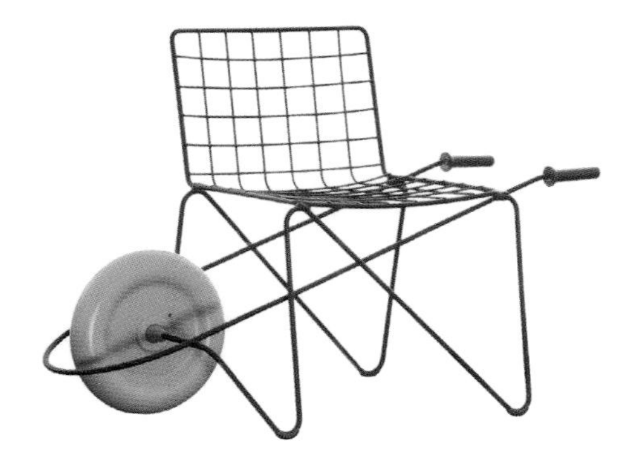

TROTTER CHAIR, ROGIER MARTENS, 2015 MAGIS ME TOO

A deliberate crossbreeding of a wheelbarrow and a chair, this ingenious seat was created by Dutch designer Rogier Martens. He is known for his playful approach and desire to interact with the user. Made of rounded green steel tubes and a rotation-molded wheel in orange, Trotter makes it easy to move it around and play with it, which is exactly what children love. Its smart construction makes it both comfortable as well as practical (weather resistant and very stable). Trotter is fun to play with.

ACAPULCO CHAIR, DESIGNER UNKNOWN, 1950S BOQA

The history of this chair's design goes back to the 1950s when Acapulco became a popular seaside resort. It is believed that a French tourist visiting the city found that solid chairs were unsuitable for the Mexican heat and so he created a lightweight construction for the tropical climate based on traditional Mayan hammocks. The kids' version of the chair is also made of vinyl cords spread over a metallic oval-shaped frame. The vinyl cords offer a super comfortable sitting experience. This chair, available in countless bright and happy colors, is particularly popular outdoors during the summer.

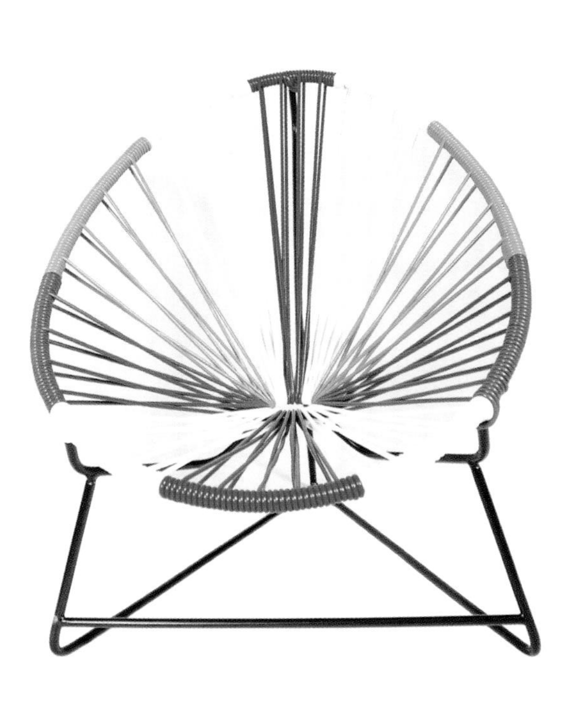

LUXEMBOURG KID COLLECTION, FERMOB

Recreating the charm of the Luxembourg garden in Paris has never been so easy. Inspired by the French capital's iconic low garden chair, the collection by Fermob (also available in an adult size) includes classic chairs, armchairs, benches, and even tables. Thanks to their lovely rounded edges, tubular bases, pleasant color palettes, and smooth finishes, pieces from the series can adorn any outdoor space as well as furnish interiors. Easy to maintain, they are made of aluminum, and are thus light to carry. Elegant and fun, the range of seats and tables can turn eating or playing into an exceptional experience.

AGATHA CHAIR AND TABLE, ÁGATHA RUIZ DE LA PRADA VONDOM

The Spanish company Vondom teamed up with the renowned Ágatha Ruiz de la Prada to design the brand's first children's collection. Made up of a table, a miniature chair, and a plant pot, it is an inventive and joyful celebration of imagination. The dynamic and inventive shapes are enhanced with vivid colors and the finest execution. The chairs take the form of stretched hearts, while the table and planter resemble flowers with wide petals. As the owner of such a fantastic set, one might feel like Alice stepping into Wonderland.

PIEDRAS COLLECTION, JAVIER MARISCAL, 2006 MAGIS ME TOO

Piedras is a series consisting of an armchair, a sofa, and a low table that can be used individually or as a sculptural ensemble. With their extraordinary shapes, gray anthracite color, and porous texture, the collection looks like furniture carved in stone, but they are made of very light and practical polyethylene. The organic forms blend into natural environments, creating a generous space for outdoor play. The manufacturer describes them as "almost like those of primitive Man, but lighter and comfier."

THE ROOF CHAIR,
SPALVIERI & DEL CIOTTO, 2018
MAGIS ME TOO

The duo Spalvieri and Del Ciotto demonstrate how fun a simple, yet ingenious idea can be. A pitched-roof-shaped frame made of aluminum tube has been covered with flexible polyurethane to inspire movement and interaction. At home or in the garden, it can be a playful seat for two (as children can occupy both elastic sides at once), adjusting perfectly to the body, or it can become a tent-like construction to play under (connecting a couple of the chairs can easily create a fascinating tunnel for children to crawl through). Pure fun!

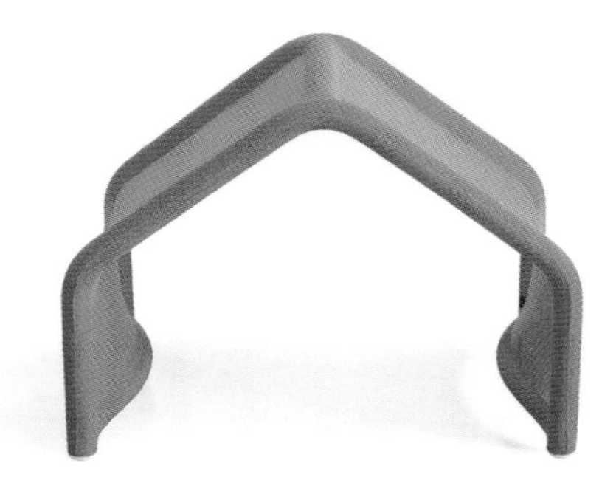

#STOOLS

Smaller yet as indispensable as chairs, stools can be used in various ways. Whether children simply sit on them, use them as a stepstool to reach something that is too high, or treat them as side tables, it is important for stools to have original shapes and to be easy to move.

LC14 TABOURET NANTES REZÉ,
LE CORBUSIER, 1952/1959 (RE-EDITED IN 2018)
CASSINA COLLEZIONE I MAESTRI

Le Corbusier designed this geometric stool for the children's bedrooms in the Nantes-Rezé apartment building. Unlike with other stools, the architect used simple right angles. These simple shapes, and varnished oak wood, give the stool a monolithic look. The combination of the typical Le Corbusier hues of pale blue and chestnut brown enhances the geometry of the stool. To make it easy to lift, the massive volume includes a rectangular opening on each side, which also makes it look like a miniature house. One of its sides opens, thus transforming LC14 into a storage bin.

CHILDREN'S STOOL NE60, ALVAR AALTO, 1934 ARTEK

In the late 1920s, Alvar Aalto, Finnish architect and designer, developed a technique for bending wood, which is demonstrated by the characteristic L-legs of this iconic stool. The four of them, like spiders' legs, are simply mounted to the round seat, resulting in a light but hardwearing structure. The solid birch it is made of gives it a natural feel, while the geometric shape of the stool allows it to be stacked into a round tower. Stable and perfectly proportioned, NE60 can become a tiny tabletop or storage unit.

ELEPHANT STOOL, SORI YANAGI, 1954 VITRA

Known for marrying western industrial design with Japan's native artisanal traditions, Sori Yanagi creates delightful designs with refined minimalism. Inspired by the shape of an elephant, the Japanese designer envisioned this adorable children's stool. Its organic forms are expressed in thin plastic with two classic color versions: black or white. The legs on three corners, rounded edges, and a slightly concave seating surface make it a useful object for everyday use as well as a toy. Inventively shaped, easy to clean, stackable, and light to carry, the Elephant achieves all the essential requirements. It is also weatherproof so it can be used outdoors.

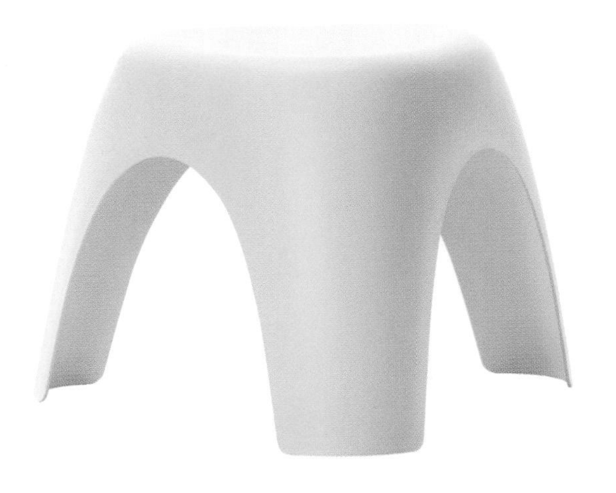

PET STOOLS, HANNA EMELIE ERNSTING PETITE FRITURE

Recognizing children's spontaneous love for animals, designers draw numerous inspirations from their shapes and patterns to come up with truly inventive designs. Stools are no exception. German designer Hanna Emelie Ernsting envisioned Daisy and Fin, two sheep-like seats. The generous use of quilted fabrics as well as the upholstered shape invites the user not only to sit but also to cuddle. Comfortable and playful, the stools are also easy to care for, as the outer shell can be removed for dry-cleaning.

BAMBI, SHEEP, AND COW STOOLS, TAKESHI SAWADA, 2014 EO

Takeshi Sawada's sculptural approach to stools has resulted in three enchanting pieces of furniture. His design principle is that objects are never only objects but must also evoke feelings. The concept is simple yet ingenious – a rounded seat is upholstered and covered with a pattern matching an animal's hide. Set on four regular legs, it also includes an amusing backrest in the form of ears or antlers. Bambi and Cow are made of European oak and American walnut, while beech wood is used for Sheep.

BOLD STOOL, BIG-GAME MOUSTACHE

Swiss design studio Big-Game takes experimenting with metal tubular structures to a new level. Bold is a funky stool made of two identical tubular steel elements nested into each other. Bold, both in name and form, this stool is inflated with polyurethane foam for maximum comfort. The graphic shape of the padding is fantastically enhanced with vibrant colors, making the stool even cooler. Not only is the design comfortable, but it is also practical – the fabric cover is removable and washable.

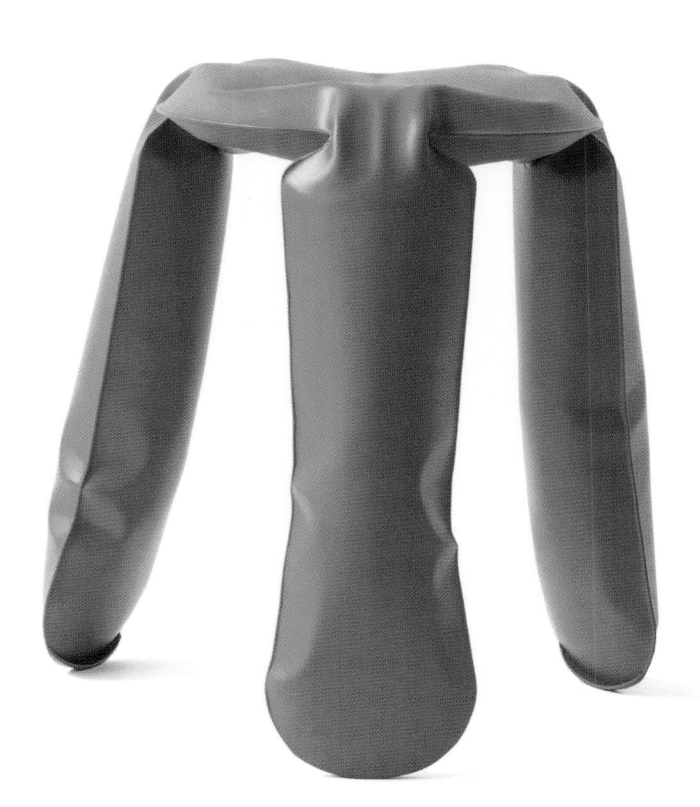

PLOPP MINI STOOL, OSKAR ZIETA, 2009 ZIETA STUDIO

Equally contorted, Plopp Mini looks like a balloon-type toy rather than a piece of furniture. Polish designer Oskar Zięta uses FIDU, an innovative technology, where "two ultra-thin steel sheets are welded together around their edges and inflated under high pressure," as he explains. The effect is a three-dimensional object that is very light but durable. Available in numerous matte and polished color versions, it also has a great optical illusion effect.

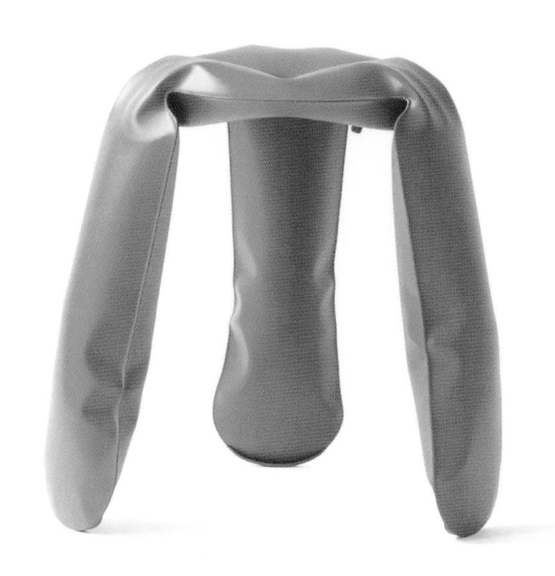

LETTER STOOLS,
SASCHA GREWE, 2011
ARTCANBREAKYOURHEART

Fascinated by the alphabet when learning to read and write, kids will be delighted to have these A-to-Z typographic stools invented by Sascha Grewe. They can be arranged in any order to form a powerful word or, even better, a child's name. The flat tops also make useful side tables, plus some of the letters offer an inner storage space in the form of a shelf or a drawer. Manufactured by hand and made of MDF, the series is varnished in a wide range of bright and happy colors.

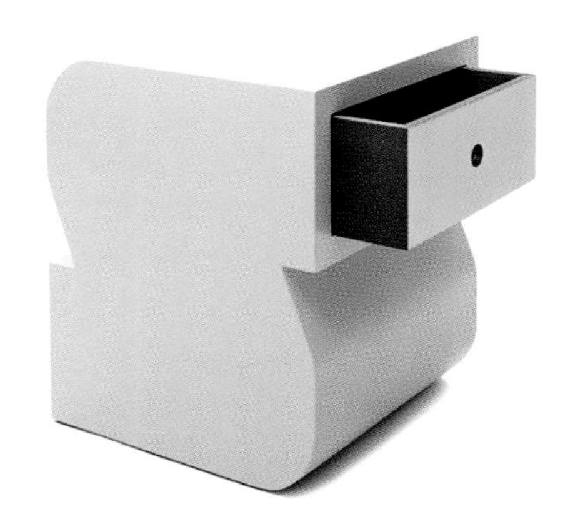

MARK

#TABLES, DESKS & SETS

Playing on the floor will always be fun, but as they get older children also start looking for a comfortable place to organize their work and play spaces. Drawing or enjoying activity books requires chairs and tables perfectly adjusted to little bodies. The heights of the seats and tabletops, as well as their shapes, are what matter most here.

RISOM CHILD'S AMOEBA TABLE, RISOM CHILD'S SIDE CHAIR, JENS RISOM, 1943 KNOLL, INC.

In Knoll's illustrious history, this particular collection is quite special as these are the very first pieces of furniture ever designed for the manufacturer. Jens Risom created a set that will add mid-century charm to any playroom. The wooden chairs are complemented with vividly hued webbing straps that are used for both the seat and backrest. The mix of solid frame and flexible elements is both visually playful and comfortable. Interestingly, the material used for the straps comes from discarded nylon from parachute factories. The Amoeba Table with its organic shape is perfect for inventive, creative activities.

PINGPONG COLLECTION, OLIVER FURNITURE

Oliver Furniture specializes in furniture for toddlers with a Nordic flair. The PingPong collection has been envisioned with the little ones in mind. It includes a table, a chair, and a stool, and can be arranged in different combinations. The design mixes oak bases with white MDF elements, which makes a natural and lovely combination. The structures, with their focus on balance, are light and easy for children to use. The seats are comfortably wide, while the egg-shaped low table can be accessed from every side.

CH410 PETER'S CHAIR AND TABLE, HANS J. WEGNER, 1944 CARL HANSEN & SØN

Humorously called by the manufacturer "furniture and a 3D puzzle in one," this set does not require tools to be assembled. The chair, made of four carefully crafted pieces of wood (untreated beech), has an adorable shape that is perfectly suited to little people. Danish architect and cabinetmaker Hans J. Wegner created it during World War II as a gift for Peter, his friend's son. The idea was to come up with a piece of furniture that would not only be functional but also stimulate the imagination. This innovative seat can be paired with Peter's Table, which is based on the same principles.

ELEPHANT CHAIR & TABLE,
MARC VENOT, 2016
EO

The Elephant Chair and Table, designed by Marc Venot for EO, are both defined by their curvaceous lines. The rounded forms speak to children's imaginations – a simple seat becomes a ride on an elephant's back, embraced by the animal's ears: for smaller children it can be a fun hideout, for older ones a comfortable back and armrests. The oval table, based on the same legs as the chair, makes a great companion. Each piece of furniture, made from fine European beech wood, is perfectly executed.

TABLE & CHAIR,
THITAREE LUENGTANGVARODOM, 2016
PLANTOYS

The playful shape of this set launched by PlanToys was made possible thanks to the use of bent wood. The chair, which is pleasantly curved, and the desk-like table are ready for active play. The table offers two solutions that all kids will enjoy. First, the tabletop is made of a blackboard surface, so children can draw on it with chalk. Second, underneath there are two shelves for storing crayons or colored paper.

GEO'S TABLE & LILLY'S CHAIR, SEBASTIAN JØRGENSEN WE DO WOOD

The Danish label We do Wood chose bamboo for their furniture because, as the manufacturer stresses, it is one of the most sustainable natural resources on the globe. Not only is it grown without pesticides, but it is also processed without the use of harmful chemicals and transformed with low formaldehyde emissions. The vintage flair of Lilly's Chair and Geo's Table is not only due to their unusual shapes, but also thanks to the interesting texture of the wood. Underneath the tabletop there is a shelf for storage, so as soon as arts and crafts activities are over, one can easily store all the materials there.

LITTLE ARCHITECT TABLE AND CHAIR, LITTLE ARCHITECT DESK FERM LIVING

"Make room for your little geniuses to shape and form ideas, throw small dinner parties, or color for hours," encourages Ferm Living, the manufacturer of this geometric set. The minimalist Little Architect collection is produced in solid ash wood and ash veneer. It includes a table, chairs, and a bench, as well as a desk, which can all be combined in various ways. To emphasize the design's elegant simplicity, this visually light series is available in a sophisticated range of soft colors.

MY LITTLE PUPITRE DESK, JUNGLE BY JUNGLE

My Little Pupitre Desk is reminiscent of a piano with a small stool. Retro in shape, this stylish set for children ages 3 to 6 doesn't take up too much space, yet it offers a great surface for all creative activities. Additionally, the solid tabletop opens easily to reveal a large box where kids can store their coloring books or pencils. Don't worry about pinched fingers: a special soft closure mechanism slows down the closing movement.

TABLE HARICOT, LAURETTE

As it is envisioned for children up to 3 years, Table Haricot proves that even the youngest ones can have a small atelier of their own. The organic shape and fancy colors provide a lovely environment for play. A storage compartment under the top is yet another nice element of this design from Laurette. Made of a combination of maritime pine and MDF, it can be complemented with a small round stool from the same collection.

LUISA TABLE AND CHARLIE CHAIR, ECOBIRDY

The eye-catching design of the Luisa Table and Charlie Chair by ecoBirdy is a successful example of innovative technology. Made of *ecothylene®*, based on recycled plastic, it is produced in a special and eco-friendly process that takes typically dull material and turns it into attractive objects. Its characteristic speckled patterns resembling the texture of marble, and its smooth surfaces, make the furniture pleasing to the eyes. To improve their ergonomic aspect, the designers focused on rounding all the edges and providing both ample seating and a generous tabletop surface. Pleasant to touch and easy to clean, light yet stable and robust, the set can be used both indoors and outdoors.

OZOO DESK AND CHAIR, MARC BERTHIER, 1968/2018 ROCHE BOBOIS

To celebrate their iconic design's 50th anniversary, the French brand Roche Bobois decided to re-issue the Ozoo desk and chair envisioned by Marc Berthier in 1968. Made of plastic and molded as one piece, it has a gelcoat finish and comes in five vivid colors. Perfect for both younger kids or teenagers, and still trendy decades after its creation, the collection remains aesthetically appealing. The bright colors enhance its joyful, rounded shape. The sturdy but light forms are perfectly comfortable and easy to maintain.

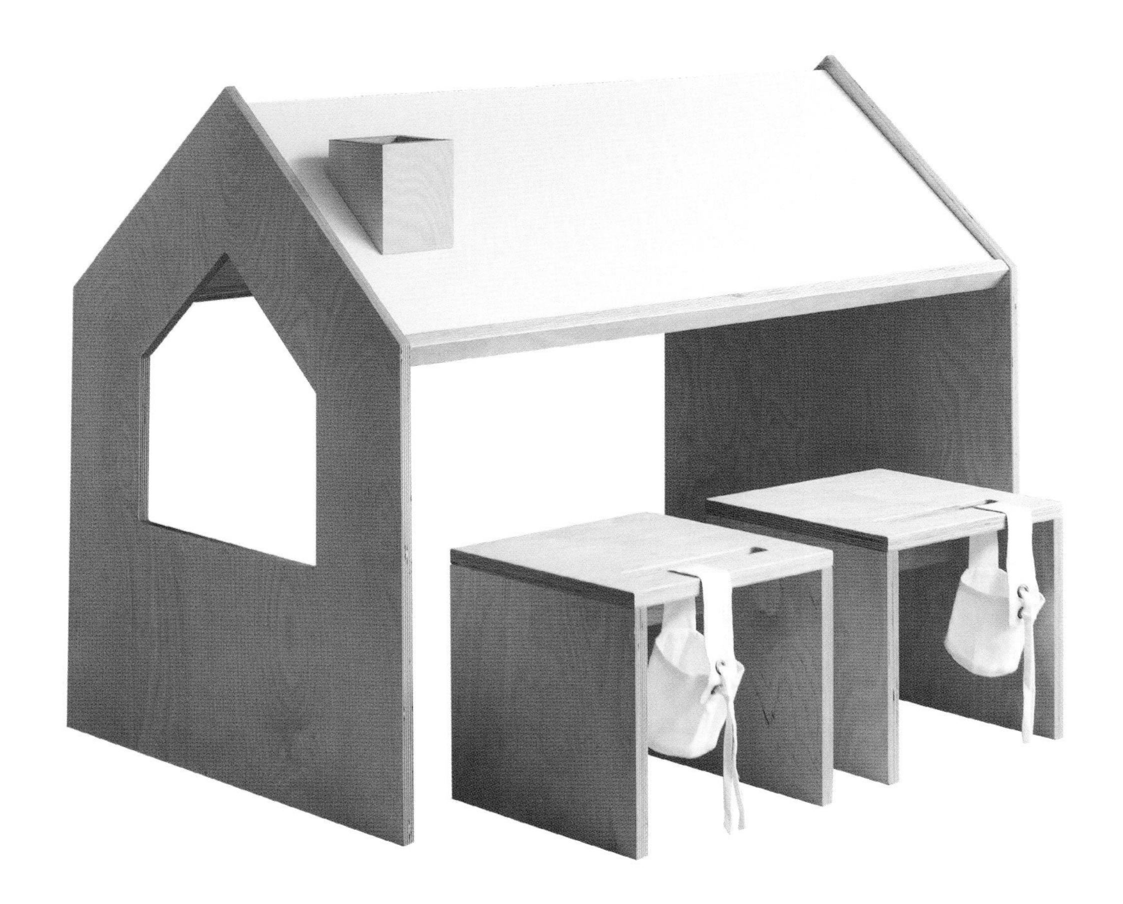

PLAYHOUSE DESK AND CHAIRS, THE ROOF® COLLECTION KUTIKAI

Hand-finished and covered with organic paint, the Playhouse desk and cubic chairs from Kutikai's portfolio are very sculptural pieces of furniture. The use of birch plywood results in a natural and light look, even though it takes up a substantial amount of space. Inspired by the schematic way children draw houses, this architectural structure sparks the imagination and can be used for more than drawing. The roof becomes a desktop (covered with white stain-resistant laminate), and the chimney can serve as a crayon box.

NOTES.

CIRCLE: KIDS' TABLE WITH 4 STOOLS, ANJA LYKKE AND EGLANTINE CHARRIER, 2012 SMALL-DESIGN

Circle, by Small-Design, in birch plywood with laminate, consists of a table that has a rather massive structure and four stools, which are lighter and more sculptural in form. Hidden under the table, they are barely visible. Geometric in shape, the stools can be arranged together in various ways. When nested, both sets are compact pieces of furniture; when in use, they form a playful space with an easily accessible table surface that can be used by several children at once.

LITTLE FLARE, MARCEL WANDERS, 2005 MAGIS ME TOO

Marcel Wanders is known for his designs with a twist. Little Flare is no exception. Its robust legs are made of transparent polycarbonate and the top is MDF with a white polymeric cover. His ingenious invention was to leave the legs open and place practical penholders into the hollows at each of the four corners in a happy orange. There are a couple of options to decorate the tops: a sketchbook with patterns to be completed and colored is available. Perfectly sized for children, it offers abundant space for scribbling and more. It can be paired with various chairs.

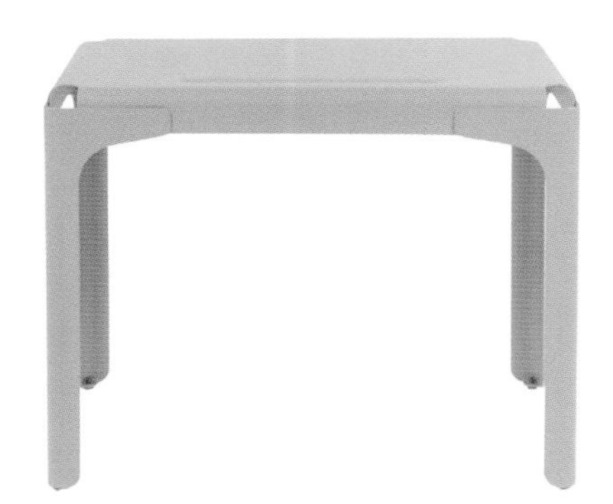

RHINO DESK, NORMAL STUDIO TOLIX®

This table by the legendary French brand Tolix®, specializing in metal furniture, successfully combines practical and aesthetical aspects. Available in a wide palette of colors, their creations look retro but have a timeless charm. The Rhino steel desk designed by Normal Studio is an example of expertly shaped metal. The robust nature of the material is counterbalanced by its slender volume and soft contours. To make it more playful, the designers added cut-outs to the corners. The desk can be paired with the Crocodile Bench from the same collection.

#CRADLES & CRIBS

As the saying goes: what youth is used to, age remembers. That is precisely why it is extremely important to ensure the proper surroundings right after the birth of a little one. Clearly, the very first piece of furniture should be a stylish cradle to provide comfort for babies during their first nights on this planet.

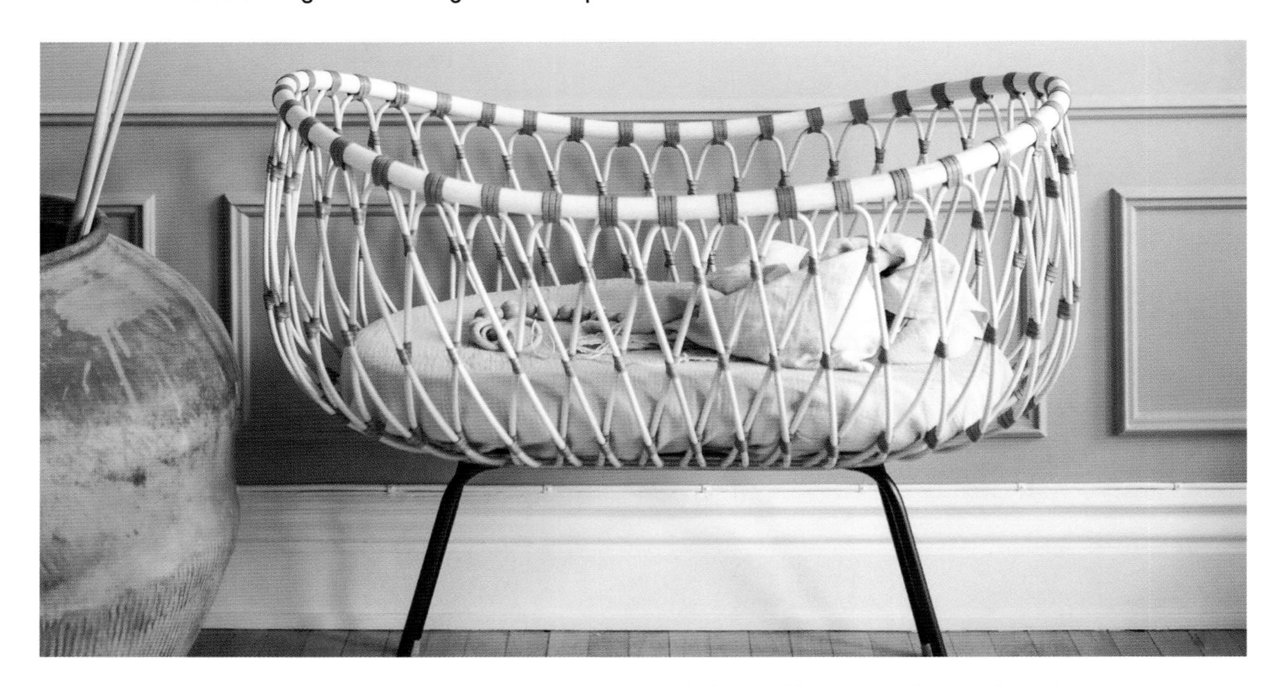

LOLA CRADLE, BERNBACH HANDCRAFTED

The light metal frame puts the visual emphasis on the baskets, which are made of stylish rattan and have beautifully woven patterns firmly laced with delicate leather straps. The shape of the legs was designed to echo the silhouette of the baskets. The parts are tied with inconspicuous screws in the thin wooden base. The transparency of the cradle's structures provides ventilation as well as the possibility for the newborn to look around and be seen. While the rounded Lola is meant for smaller babies, up to 12 months old, Frederick is ideal for little ones up to age 3. Rectangular and suspended closer to the floor, it may seem slightly heavier, but it will last longer.

FREDERICK CRADLE,
BERNBACH HANDCRAFTED

BAUHAUS CRADLE, PETER KELER, 1923 TECTA

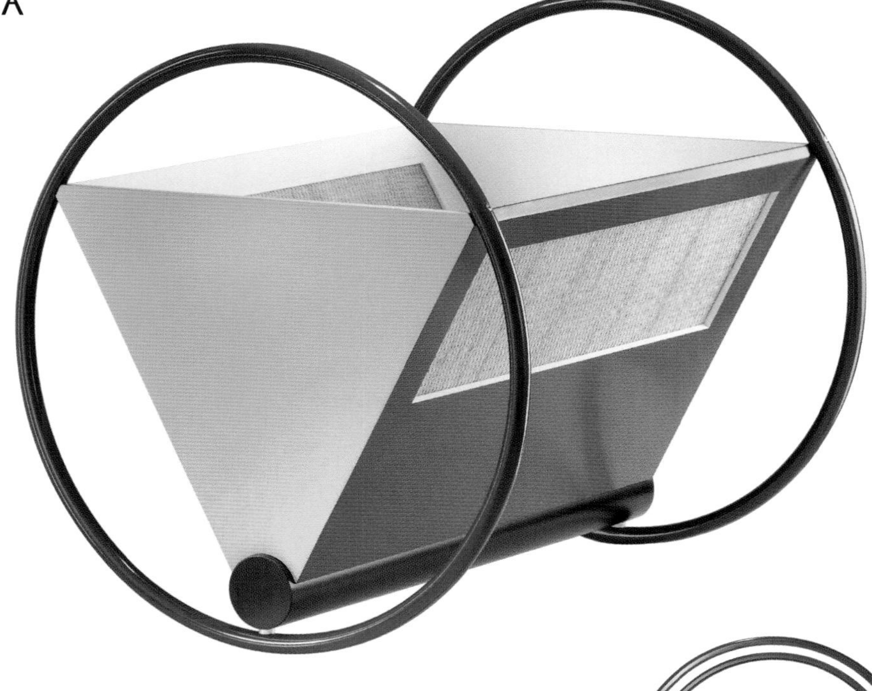

The Bauhaus Cradle, a lesser-known icon of the movement, was envisioned by Peter Keler as an entry for a furniture competition organized by Walter Gropius to design beds for a man, a woman, and a toddler. A floating, rocking, and rolling object, and as such quintessentially "Bauhaus-esque," the cradle's form is striking. Two dominating metal circles hold a V-shaped cradle that can be easily set into motion. A discreet cylinder on the bottom stabilizes the structure. The elements of the cradle marked in blue, yellow, and red draw from Wassily Kandinsky's color theory.

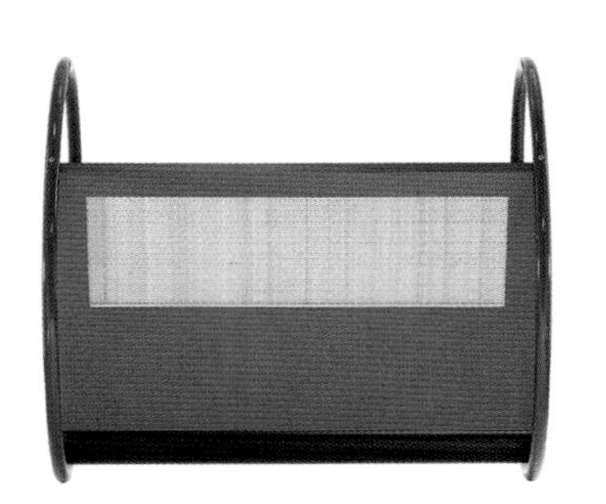

LULU CRADLE, NANNA DITZEL, 1963/2011 (LIMITED EDITION) BRDR. KRÜGER

The Lulu Cradle, designed in 1963 by renowned Danish designer Nanna Ditzel, was created for her own children and named after one of her daughters. The manufacturer Brdr. Krüger relaunched the design in 2011 to produce a limited edition of 200 pieces. Each is numbered and built of the highest quality beech wood. The cradle comes with a mattress made of 100% organic kapok, which is hypo-allergenic and water-resistant. The ergonomic shape makes it easy to swing, which babies particularly like.

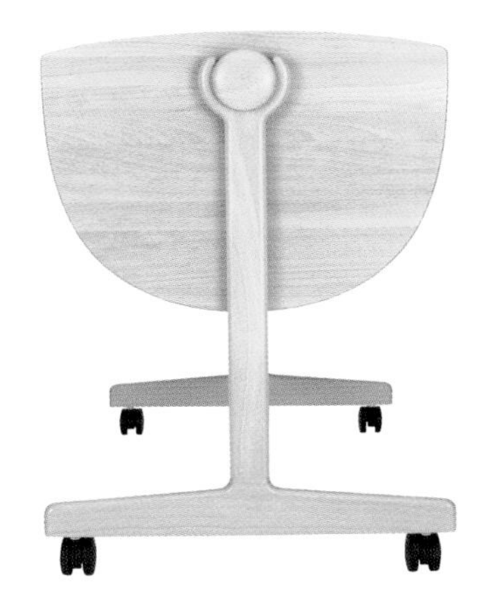

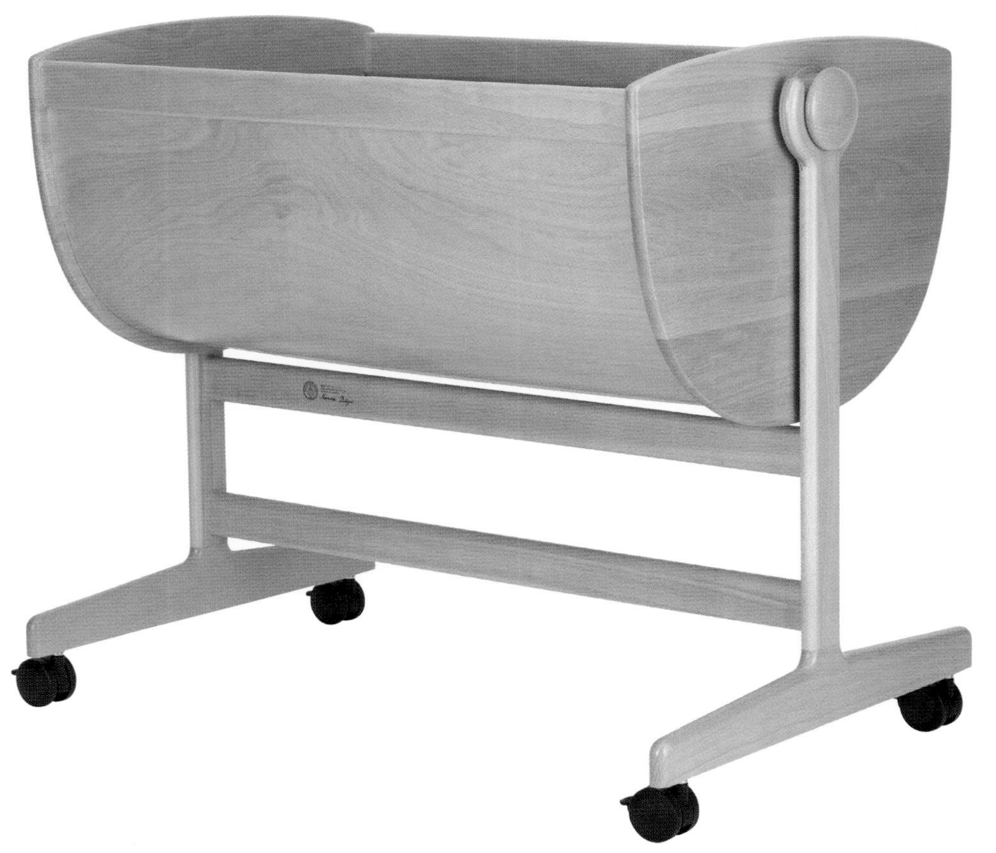

BORIS, VLADIMIR & ALEXANDER CRADLES, NIKA ZUPANC, 2009

"Imagine the good old cradle, extinct for a while and now coming back again, stylishly reincarnated in the form of a flawless holding device for ultra-young human bodies," muses Nika Zupanc, known for marrying simplicity with elegance and ingenious forms. The designer's stylish crib has a simple yet solid structure for rocking a baby gently and comes in several variations from transparent to black. It is suitable for little ones who are not yet able to sit, roll over, kneel, or pull themselves up.

SNOO CRIB, YVES BÉHAR, 2016 HAPPIEST BABY

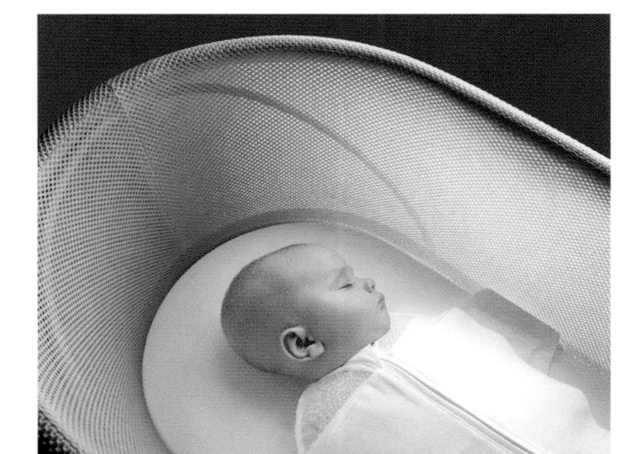

To help new parents struggling with sleep deprivation, Yves Béhar and his team at fuseproject envisioned a crib that uses advanced technology. In a 5-year collaboration with pediatrician Dr. Harvey Karp, they developed SNOO, which they call "the world's safest baby bed," which reacts to a baby's cries and movements. The innovative, curved bassinet is equipped with microphones that detect the baby's cry, while below the mattress there are sensors and speakers, plus a robotic engine that responds by creating a swinging motion. In addition, it also collects data. A special app allows parents to monitor details about their baby's sleep.

POPOP BED, EMMANUEL GALLINA AMPM

The Popop bed is an evolving structure. Designed by Emmanuel Gallina for AMPM, this ingenious bed transforms as the child grows (the wooden side barriers that keep the child safely inside the bed are removable). Interesting in shape, it nurtures the imagination and creates an intimate space for the child. Solid and playful, it is a fancy and cozy nest, whether for an early stage or later, when open sides create an unusual shape with high backrests on either end.

LA ROULOTTE CRADLE, LAURETTE

Like the Lulu Cradle, La Roulotte from Laurette is equipped with four wheels, so babies can be rocked and fall asleep more easily or can be moved around as necessary. Suitable for ages 0 to 4, the cradle's design was inspired by an Alsace cart. According to the manufacturer, it is "an invitation to travel to the planet of dreams." La Roulotte comes in a range of distinctive hues, which emphasize its retro shape. The quite massive structure is softened by its nicely rounded edges.

STOKKE® SLEEPI™ MULTIFUNCTIONAL BED, SUSANNE GRØNLUND AND CLAUS HVIID KNUDSEN STOKKE

At the core of this unique concept is practicality. It is designed to grow with the child in the first three years of life, and with a special extension it can be used even up to age 10! While it maintains its cozy oval shape, it adapts to changing needs. At each stage, one side of the bed can be removed to allow easy access. The mattress height can be easily adjusted to make it easier to put down and pick up the baby, while lockable wheels allow it to be moved between rooms.

STOKKE® SLEEPI™ MULTIFUNCTIONAL BED, SUSANNE GRØNLUND AND CLAUS HVIID KNUDSEN STOKKE

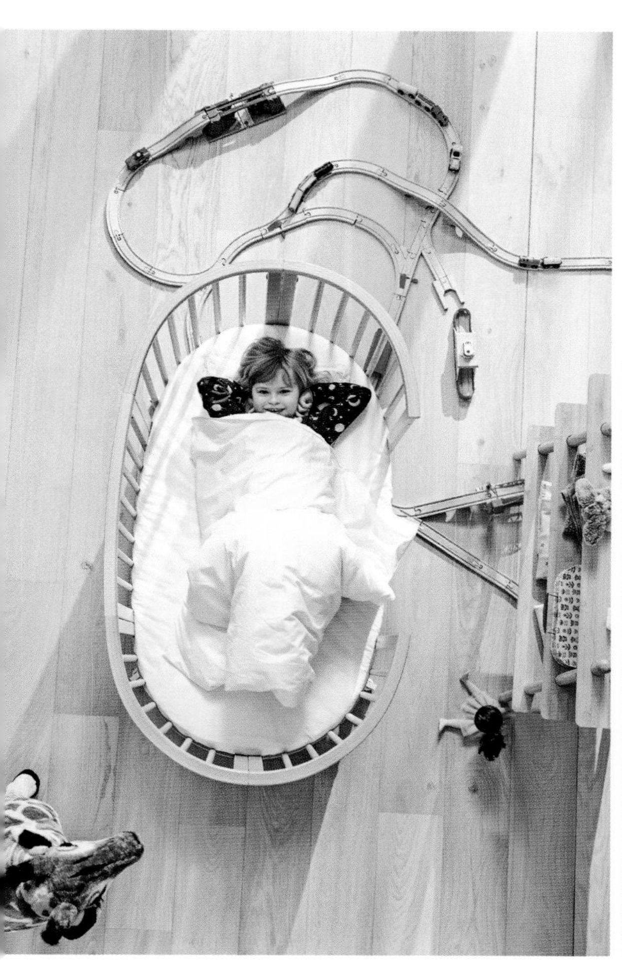

#BEDS

As soon as newborns outgrow their cribs, they need a proper bed upgrade. It is not so easy to find a design that is comfortable, safe, and fancy at the same time. We have found several great options where quickly growing offspring can relax and dream.

ECHO TODDLER BED, KALON STUDIOS

The first thing that comes to mind when looking at the Echo Toddler Bed is its solidity. The sculpted shape is made of maple and is reminiscent of an old cradle. It was designed to offer a comfortable and cozy space and to take up as little floorspace in the room as possible. Visually, this effect is achieved by its gently softened edges. The bed is low, thus making it easy to climb into or out of, while the higher sides on each end create a nest-like effect. It's the perfect mix of modern shape and traditional material.

R TODDLER BED, AGATA AND AREK SEREDYN RAFA-KIDS

Envisioned for children over 3 years old, R Toddler Bed has two main features. With safety in mind, the manufacturer has included elevated sides that offer a protective embrace but do not obstruct the view (oblong openings also make the construction look light). The second revelation is the two distinctive wheels, meaning that the bed can be easily moved around (it is fun to be able to re-arrange the room at will). Extremely strong, the bed is slightly higher than average, so the space underneath it can be used for storage.

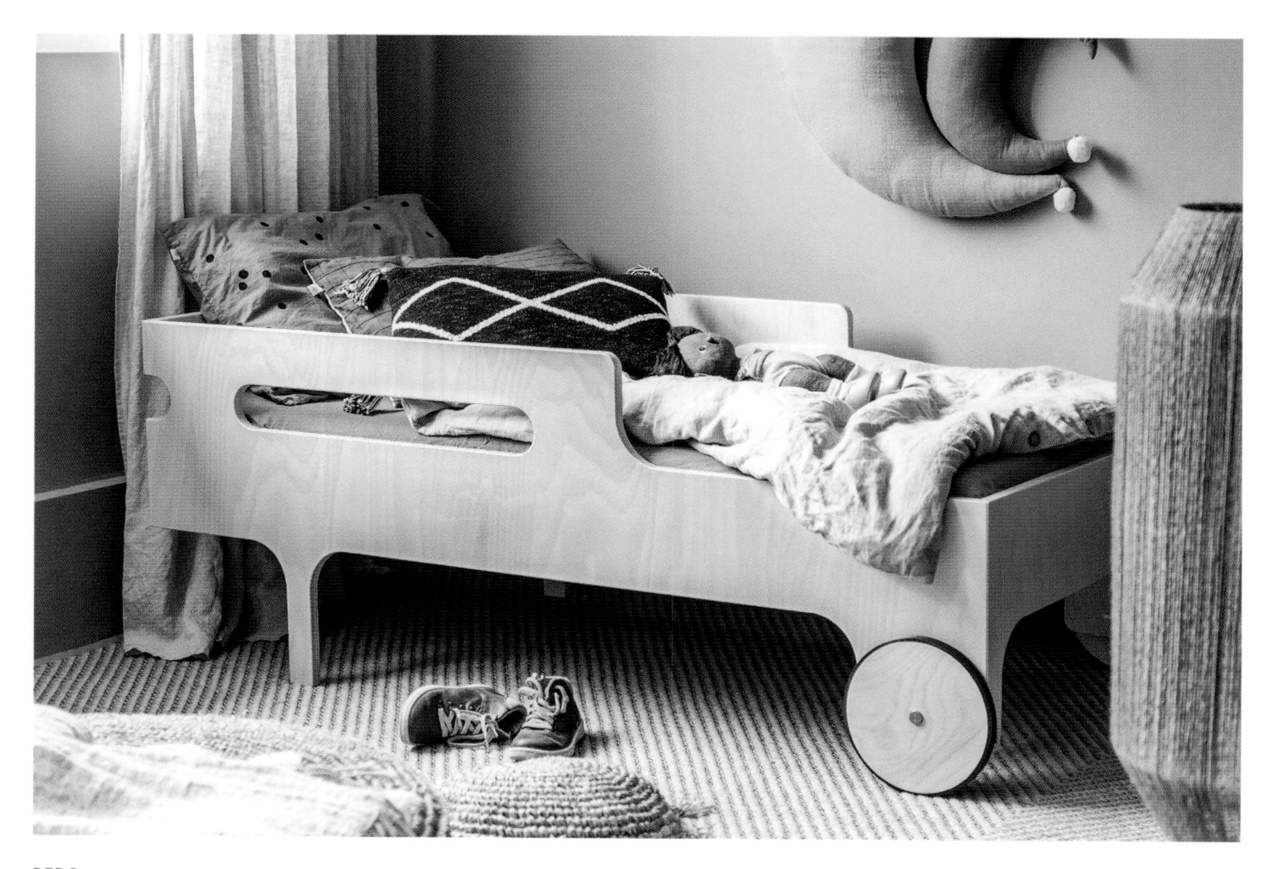

MM BED, LAURETTE

The cartoon-style MM Bed from Laurette has charming legs, a trapezoid head, and rounded contours. This shape gives it a retro flair. With lots of pillows it can alternatively serve as a sofa. The bed comes in three colors (charcoal, gray, and beige), which emphasize its distinctive yet fanciful form. For sleepover fans, the manufacturer offers an optional bed drawer that fits neatly under the bed and has an additional mattress. It is meant for children in the transitional age between childhood and adolescence.

PILE OU FACE BUNK BED, LAURETTE

This design by Laurette with its vintage look proves that space constraints should not limit parents' imagination. The manufacturer stylishly demonstrates that functional solutions can also be visually attractive. Nearly square in shape, this chic structure is available in a palette of deep, gentle colors that enhance and decorate the room. The short legs and the ladder are made in contrasting natural wood. The upper level is suitable for children over 6 years old.

BUNKY BED,
MARC NEWSON, 2012
MAGIS ME TOO

"Kids like to have fun. They like their privacy and they like to feel safe – preferably all at the same time," comments Marc Newson, the designer of this thrilling bunk bed. Made of modular plastic, it looks like an XXL toy. The block-like elements and vivid colors enhance its distinctive shape, which is a perfect hide-away or place to rest after a busy day. Interestingly, Bunky's stackable elements do not need additional fixings. It can also be easily re-arranged into two individual beds by removing the middle section.

IO BUNK POD BED, MINA PANIC AND CARLO FILIPO NEGRI, 2013 IO KIDS DESIGN

At the core of IO Bunk Pod's design was to use a minimum number of components and allow a maximum number of transformations. Primarily a double-decker, it can become a set of two separate single beds, a top bed with a generous desk area below, or a regular single bed and desk. It can successfully grow with the child, playing a different role at each stage. The designers have made the construction light and rounded. Many of the elements have openings, while each end of the bed is equipped with practical shelves.

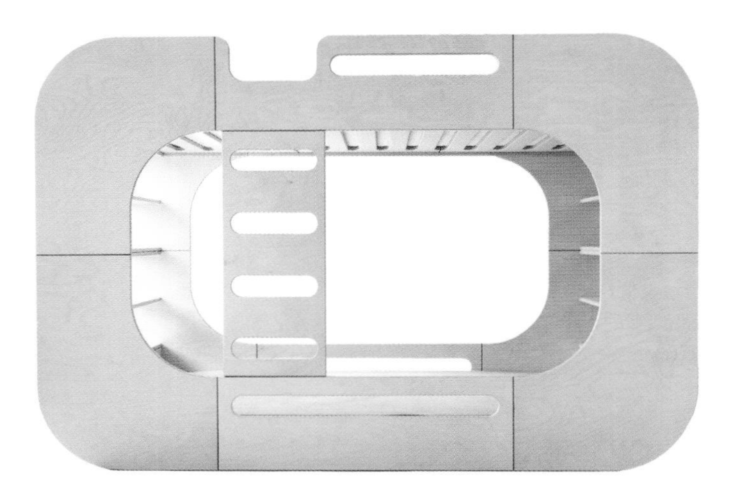

DREAM CLOUD LOFT BED, TOTEM ITALIA PLYROOM

"Sharing a bedroom is no problem," assures Plyroom, the manufacturer of this sophisticated bed. Nor, it seems, is having a small room. With the Dream Cloud Loft Bed there is plenty of space for playing or learning beneath the sleeping zone. The lightweight structure, made of birch, has a toy-like character. The ladder was designed to discourage toddlers from accessing the top of the bed. It can be paired with the Dream Cloud or the Singolo Bed from Plyroom's collection with the choice of either an L-shape or the bunk arrangement underneath.

WOOD LOFT BED, OLIVER FURNITURE

A similar solution but with an entirely different aesthetic can be found in Oliver Furniture's portfolio. The elevated bed leaves plenty of space below. Small benches and shelves can be complemented with a small table, an armchair, or a floor cushion to transform it into a compact kingdom that doesn't require extensive floor area. It is available in all-white or in a white and Nordic oak combination. If an extra bed is suddenly needed in the children's room, this model can easily convert into an elegant bunk bed.

TODDLER BED,
THE ROOF® COLLECTION
KUTIKAI

Toddler Bed from The Roof® Collection is wide and quite low to give children the freedom to climb in and out of it. At the head there is a rather gigantic structure resembling a house with window openings. Serving as an embracing shelter at night, it can inspire various games or offer a fantastic reading space during the day. The other end is finished with a shelf-like element that can also be used as a mini tabletop. The fancy structure is an ode to plywood.

BEECH WOOD HOUSE BED, THÉLISSA DESHAYES BONNESOEURS®

Imagine a dollhouse where your children will spend magical nights. The shape of a house often inspires the design of beds, a perfect idea if we think of a bed as a kind of hideout and private space. The French brand Bonnesoeurs® created the iconic Beech Wood House Bed as a simple pitched roof structure. Sitting directly on the floor, it has a slatted base to allow for better air circulation under the mattress. The top part is perfect for adding decorative elements, such as lights or fabrics. The minimalist structure can also be used as a play zone when assembled without the base.

BUN VAN BED

FANTASY AIR BALLOON BED

SKY B PLANE BED

CIRCU

Children like anything extraordinary. After the numerous ingenious designs featured on the previous pages, the cherry on top is this collection from CIRCU. The label offers themed kids' beds in quite magical versions. Whether it is the round Fantasy Air Balloon with its impressive structure up to the ceiling (used as lighting), a Bun Van inspired by the iconic 60's camper van Fillmore from the Disney movie "Cars" (its interior includes several storage compartments, a TV, a desk, a mini bar, and a sofa), or the Sky B Plane, each of them can inspire children's imaginations and encourage their adventurous spirits. All the models are extraordinary elements of room decoration. It's true, these luxury toy-like pieces of furniture require a lot of space and a big budget, but they are carefully considered down to the tiniest detail and executed with outstanding quality.

#SHELVES

For all their books and toys, children need nice shelves. The ideal shelf should be an innovative design that is practical, yet that also stands out in the space. Whether it hangs on a wall or stands against one, it should have an interesting shape – as if it were a shelf from *Alice in Wonderland*.

BOOKWORM SHELF, RON ARAD, 1993 KARTELL

Tel-Aviv-born and London-based designer Ron Arad invented this whimsical shelf resembling a caterpillar. What a perfect idea for young bookworms! Produced by Kartell, it can be shaped like a snake or a spiral, or in any other curving configuration. Thanks to this flexible structure, it forms the most unusual patterns on the wall. Dynamic as the Bookworm shelf seems, it is also very stable and safe. Books and toys resting on its bending lines defy gravity. This controlled chaos has a truly artistic look.

SKATEBOARD SHELVES, LEÇONS DE CHOSES

The French brand Leçons de Choses understands kids and teenagers very well. Their iconic Skateboard shelves are pieces of decoration that stimulate the imagination and memories. The brilliant idea to base the shape on that of a classic skateboard introduces streetstyle into children's rooms. The vintage look and vivid colors are the strong points of the series. It can be arranged to form a multi-level shelving system or a single focal point on the wall. The shelves are also available in a version that includes a lamp.

R A F
Bruno Munari's
ABC
Semplice lezione di inglese
Paul
Klee
for children
25
2
Mee met de
paraplu

XL SHELF,
AGATA AND AREK SEREDYN
RAFA-KIDS

While the previous design took the form of a skateboard, this shelf resembles the curves of a skate park. Imaginatively shaped, it can become a truly playful display. Delicate metallic elements at the front make sure nothing falls from the shelves. It is particularly useful for storing a collection of plush toys. Books can be stored decoratively with their covers facing out. With their various heights, the shelves can be creatively arranged. Made of Finnish Birch plywood, the XL Shelf comes in an all-white version or a white backboard and natural wood version.

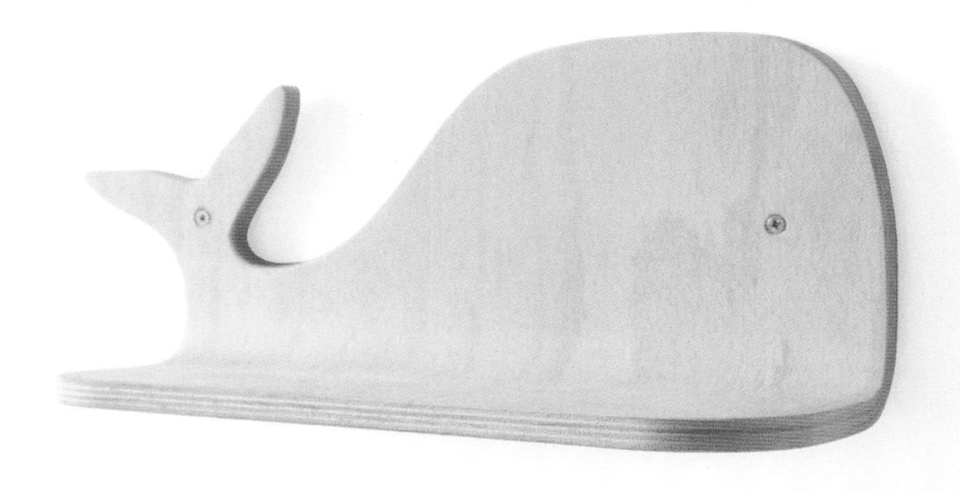

WHALE SHELF, LAETITIA OLSAK AND CLOTILDE LE THÉO, 2016 MUM AND DAD FACTORY

This design from Mum and Dad Factory is a whale-shaped wooden shelf that is fixed with screws directly to the wall. The smooth, raw-moulded beech plywood is shaped to focus on the whale's form, while the shelf itself seems to disappear. While made for storing objects, it can also be a nice decoration for the wall when empty. The natural material with its unique wood grain pattern will look great against any color or wallpaper motif. The series of shelves by the same manufacturer also includes a mountain, a cloud, a rock, and a house.

ISOLA SHELF, STUDIO BRICHET ZIEGLER MOUSTACHE

The practical side of shelves for little ones is important, especially when those rooms are filled with blocks, figurines, and numerous objects. Since children are natural collectors, they need ingenious solutions to organize their precious belongings. A set of three ceramic shelves designed by Studio Brichet Ziegler for Moustache is just right – the irregular ovals fixed directly to the wall look whimsical and can be freely adjusted to fit any space. Available either as a set or as individual shelves, in several subtle hues, Isola can also be successfully used in other rooms.

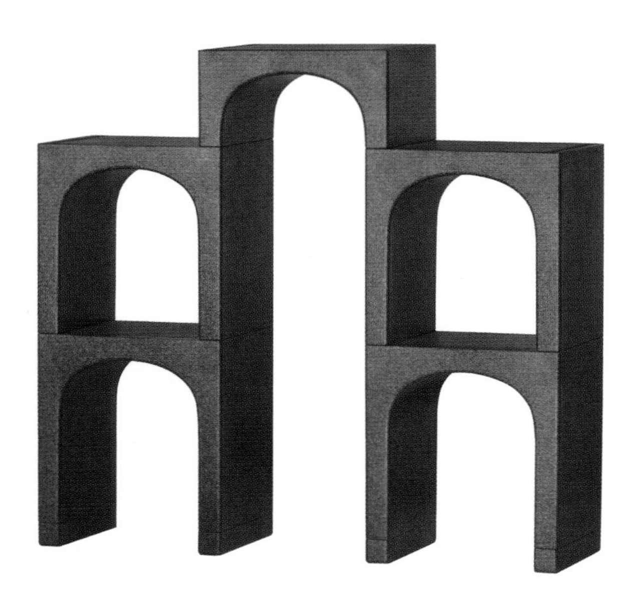

EUR SHELVES,
GIULIO IACCHETTI, 2013
MAGIS ME TOO

The modular system created by Italian designer Giulio Iacchetti is called EUR and can be easily extended both upwards and sideways. The shape of the modules was inspired by the Square Colosseum (the Palazzo della Cività Italiana) that was originally built for the 1942 Universal Exposition planned for the EUR quarter of Rome (never held because of WWII). Stacked and adjoined to compose an innovative shelving system, the components can be arranged in various configurations and creatively adjusted to any space. Architecture within a room!

UN
LIBRO
GRUFFALÒ
LE STORIE DELLA BUONANOTTE
DI MAMMA OCA
Dov'è Orso?

LADRILLOS SHELVES, JAVIER MARISCAL, 2005 MAGIS ME TOO

The shelving system Ladrillos, designed by Javier Mariscal, combines utility with an original aesthetic. The long, well-spaced shelves are ready to hold lots of toys and books, supported by sculptures of hilarious creatures in vivid colors (two on each level). Looking as if they escaped from a cartoon movie, they turn this simple and minimalist structure into an extraordinary bookshelf. To make the composition even more decorative, the white shelves are finished with black edges. The construction is fun and visually light. Ladrillos is double-sided and ideal for dividing space in a subtle way.

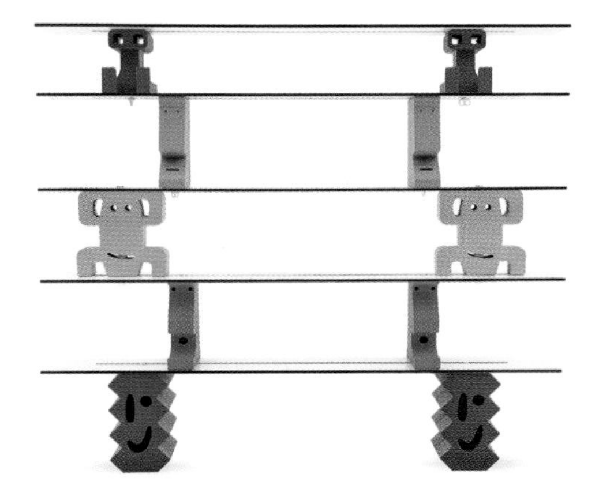

LA FOLIE BOOKSHELF, LAURETTE

Looking like a combination of a ladder and some shelves, the bookshelf La Folie (Madness) is made of five cubic elements, each with different dimensions. Arranged in an artistically chaotic way and fixed to the wall with only two metallic sticks, these shelves seem to float in the air. The forms are clearly well balanced, and the design is as decorative as it is practical. The generously spaced compartments offer numerous ways of displaying items, while the overall structure looks very light.

KIDS' BOOKCASE, ANJA LYKKE AND EGLANTINE CHARRIER, 2012 SMALL-DESIGN

The concepts from Small-Design's portfolio are characterized by great practicality. This Kids' Bookcase is yet another good example. Not only does it fit in a corner to create spacious storage, but it also has shelves that are easily accessible. Its rounded trapezoidal shape nicely fills the corner while the shelves open into the interior. Braced between the walls, it is perfectly stable without any risk of tipping over. And when the book or toy collections grow, two bookcases can be put together to form a half circle against a wall, doubling the number of shelves.

ABRIL TREE, STUDIOLAV FOR CURLY

Inspired by wooden puzzle games, the Abril Tree is made up of a series of flat elements that create a complex 3D structure when arranged together, which can be built by children and their parents. The profiles reproducing foliage were designed to refer to the four seasons of the year, but the structure is adjustable and can be easily personalized by rearranging the profiles. The designer's goal was to make it an all-in-one playground, creative hub, and starting point for adventure.

DOWNTOWN SHELF, OIVA TOIKKA, 2011 MAGIS ME TOO

Oiva Toikka was inspired by architecture when designing his shelf for Magis Me Too's children's collection. Drawing from the shapes of Manhattan skyscrapers, the designer superimposed five stacked elements, which get smaller towards the top, with a total height of over 5'10'' (180 cm.). All three sides, in matte white, are richly textured to suggest regular and endless windows. As such, it is extremely decorative and can stand freely. Made of polyethylene, and manufactured using the rotational molding technique, it is suitable for outdoor use.

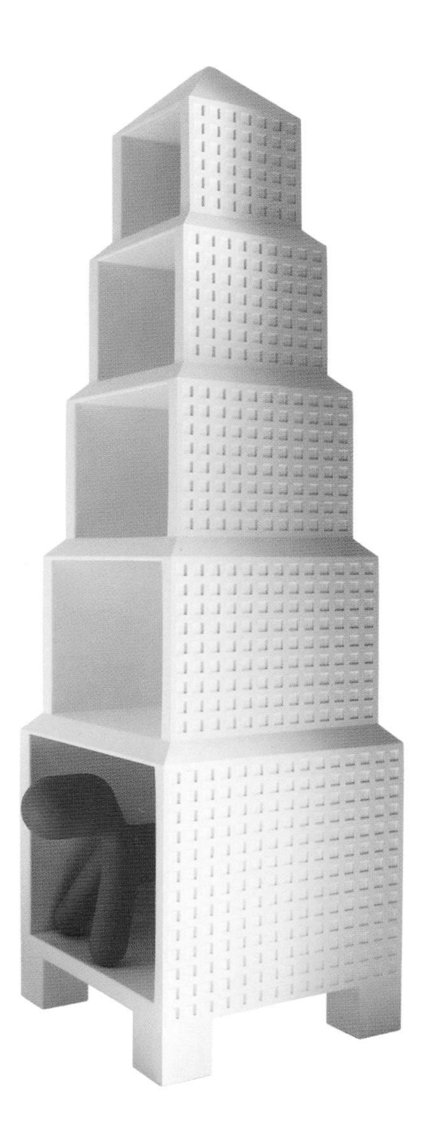

#STORAGE

Not everything has to be put on display. Children's rooms are full of items, often very tiny ones, that require proper storage space, and which are easy to hide from view. These modules also act as treasure boxes, so it is important to find the right format.

COMPONIBILI SMILE STORAGE MODULE, FABIO NOVEMBRE KARTELL

Fabio Novembre gives a new face, quite literally, to the iconic Componibili designed by Anna Castelli Ferrieri in 1967. Representing flexibility and practicality, it has remained a timeless storage module for decades. Fueled by the imagery we know from emojis, the new version is a happy smiling face. It is made up of two compartments, the top of which features eyes and the bottom one the smile. Still perfectly functional, this molded plastic cylinder was given a funny expression. The design is available in three different smile versions, offering even more fun.

PETIT ROBOT BEDSIDE CABINET, LAURETTE

The Petit Robot Bedside Cabinet, like the previous design, can be used as a bedside table with a surface on the top and a practical drawer. Four solid feet serve as the base for the rather massive top in a surprising structure that does indeed have a robotic quality. Its solid look is softened by smooth edges, which also gives it some vintage flair. It goes perfectly with other pieces of furniture from Laurette's collection, but it can also be a strong single accent in a room.

TURTLE TOY CHEST, NORMAL STUDIO TOLIX®

All parents know how important it is to equip a child's room with a spacious box that can contain everything that would otherwise cover the floor, especially those tiny blocks that nobody likes stepping on. Here we have two aesthetically different but very practical solutions. Normal Studio created their vintage style Turtle Toy Chest for Tolix®. It is made of aluminum and comes in a wide range of hues, making it easy to adjust to the room's décor. Its shape is delineated with rounded corners and an elegant, thin silhouette. The lack of any side openings makes it a rather static piece of furnishing. To create his egg-shaped container, Javier Mariscal worked with polyethylene. Despite its relatively large dimensions, the volume is light and thanks to discrete openings on the sides, it is also easy to move around. The matte white surface is textured in a pattern resembling a golf ball.

EL BAÚL TOY CHEST, JAVIER MARISCAL, 2005 MAGIS ME TOO

AGATA
G
PAPA
MAMMA

HOUSE TOY BOX
LITTLE BIG ROOM BY DJECO

The French brand Djeco is known for ingenious toys that develop skills and imagination. Some of them can be very practical, like this House Toy Box, which children can use for play and then to clean up their rooms before bedtime. Covered with charming, colorful patterns imitating the walls of a house, it is covered with a trapezoid top. The handle straps on two sides and a Velcro strip that fastens on the "roof" make it easy to carry and close. Additionally, this box is easily foldable, so it can be stored flat at times when it is not needed.

SOÙ THE TURTLE BOX

EIRIS THE HEDGEHOG BOX
ALINEA MINI

Rattan is a charming and elegant material that is more and more frequently used for manufacturing various pieces of furnishing. Thanks to its flexibility, it is particularly suitable for small storage boxes in inventive shapes. Alinea Mini offers lovely boxes in the shapes of various animals to kindle the imagination. They are perfect for storing not only toys, but also extra blankets or pillows. They are big enough to be a nice decorative element and at the same time another toy in the room. The rattan structures are extremely light, so they can easily be moved around the house. For younger children some of them, like the turtle, can also act as a fanciful pouf. Their neutral colors and timeless look will make them work well with any kind of interior design.

C
Au monde
Rascal
LES MAINS DE PAPA

ACCESSORIES

#RUGS

The floor is probably the coolest place to play. With toys scattered everywhere and lots of space to play in, it is a real kingdom (adults are strictly forbidden). Not all floors are friendly enough for long-lasting occupancy, however. To make it safe and comfortable, you need a proper rug. It can't be just any rug: it should be one that is imaginative and breaks new ground (literally).

ZEBRA RUG,
LES GRAPHIQUANTS, 2017

PANDA RUG,
STUDIO TWICE, 2017
EO

EO has produced a series of rugs inspired by iconic animals from various continents. While the Zebra Rug, designed by Les Graphiquants, celebrates Africa, the Panda Rug from the Paris-based Studio Twice is a paean to Asia. The designers play with the zebra's irregular stripes and the panda's cute patches. The shapes and patterns of the animals are perfectly adjusted to the form of a rug. They are made of 100% soft, thick New Zealand wool and will surely provide warmth and coziness for the little floor occupants.

SMILE LIKE A LLAMA WASHABLE RUG, MR. WONDERFUL X LORENA CANALS, SWEET & COZY COLLECTION LORENA CANALS

Llamas are among children's most favorite animals. They have an unusual shape and interesting fur, and they behave in funny ways. All that makes them a perfect motif for a lovely, soft rug. The llama's bright smile is enhanced by pastel hues, which create a calm and pleasant playing area in a room. No need to worry about stains, though, as the rug is washable. Handmade of bio-cotton and using natural dyes, it is also eco-friendly. Children will really feel like smiling like a llama.

ELEPHANT RUG, PILEPOIL, 2013

Depending on the child's age as well as the room's style, some will choose a fluffy rug while others will prefer a flat one. The Elephant Rug by Pilepoil is something for the first group. The texture in dark gray is so soft and rich that one wants to caress it or just stretch out on it. It is perfect for all floor-based activities, inspiring additional games with its imaginative and appealing shape. Additionally, a practical laminate backing provides a nonslip surface. The French brand Pilepoil, established in 2003, uses high quality faux fur, often mixed with silk or cotton, to produce the softest rugs ever.

Rugs from the French brand Little Cabari are known for their sophistication, high quality craftsmanship, and successful melding of art and design. Nature is the main source of inspiration for the designers who, influenced by plant and animal shapes, transform them into the most adorable pieces of furnishing. The Tilky rug, made of eucalyptus fiber, depicts a sleeping fox in a cozy, round position. The soft woolen Cardinal is based on the vividly colored bird and is embossed, which enhances the visual effect. These creatures become joyful companions for children's games. Both motifs are designed in France and produced in Portugal. Each rug is available in three different sizes or can be custom-made to any specific dimensions. The brand also offers a palette of 145 colors in wool and 90 colors in eucalyptus to choose from. The label's statement claims that "Little Cabari knows how to make children and their parents dream," and it is quite true.

TILKY REDHEAD RUG

CARDINAL RUG,
CAMILLE BAZIL
AND ALICE RICARD
LITTLE CABARI

KARABE RUG

VALSO RUG, ALINEA MINI

For anyone who would like to create their own universe with smaller and colorful, imaginative rugs, Alinea Mini offers a series including a turtle and a fish. The combination of their precise drawings and vintage palette of hues make them stand out. Made of cotton, they are durable yet delicate at the same time. Given their original shapes they are also suitable as bedside rugs. Whether as a vibrant composition or used individually, the rugs from this collection will look very decorative, particularly on a wooden floor.

ANIMAL PUZZLE RUG, ART FOR KIDS BY AFKLIVING

Instead of hesitating about which animal to select for your child's rug, why not pick up a ready-made artistic collage and adopt a rug covered with wildly colorful animal motifs? Rebecca Jones decided to draw inspiration from a jungle theme and bring some exotic plants and animals into children's rooms. AFKliving envisioned a playful visual illusion, where the surface is filled with the shapes of various animals hidden within a rich pattern. Each in a different hue, they become visible from various angles, so it is fun to move around this rug and explore the contrasts to find all of them.

The Pedro and Mr. Fox Denim rugs use a single animal-shaped motif, in this case a penguin or a fox, to create a graphic pattern against a contrasting solid-color background. With an unconventional approach to the composition, they are arranged into three lines and repeated in a humorous and surprising way to avoid regularity. Playing with a simple element is thus lively and fun. Hand-woven in pure wool, these rugs are an extremely stylish addition to any room with a Scandinavian flair.

MR. FOX DENIM RUG, SCION

PEDRO RUG,
SCION

BLUE HOPSCOTCH RUG, ART FOR KIDS BY AKFLIVING

SALEON HOPSCOTCH RUG, ALINEA MINI

Playing hopscotch is one of children's favorite activities. They usually gather outdoors, draw the pattern on the pavement with chalk, and take joy in jumping. Designers make it possible to do the same at home, which is precious particularly on rainy days. Instead of scribbling on the floor, the rug provides a ready-made pattern for indoor jumping. It inspires an outdoor playground atmosphere within the four walls and, by simple means, transforms the floor in an inventive way.

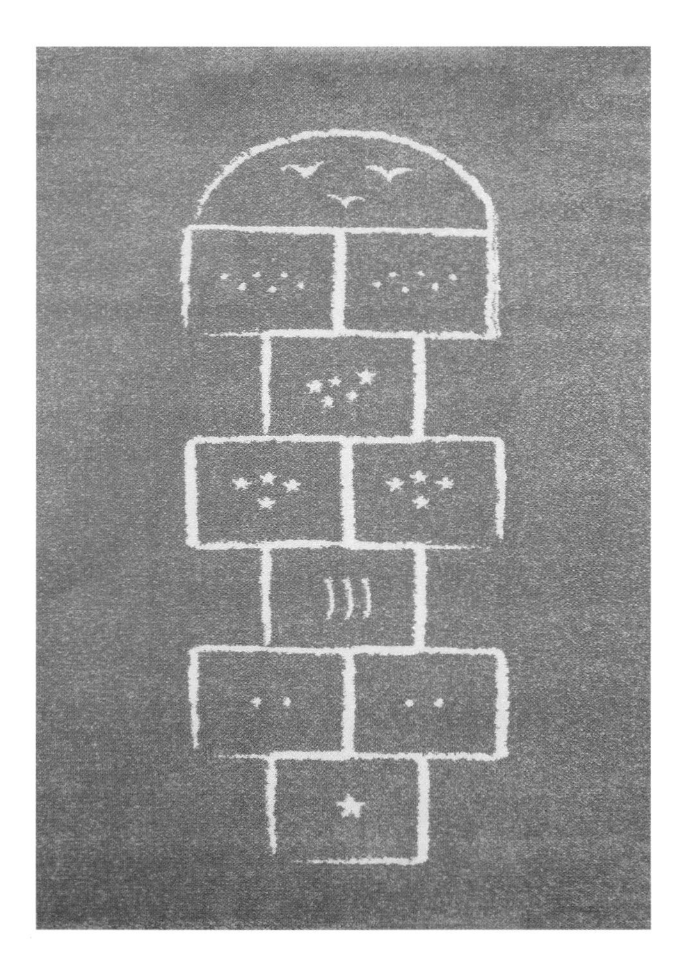

SKY RUG, CIRCU

The sky is a subject that fascinates both children and designers. The continuously changing forms of clouds and shades of blue have inspired many pieces of furnishing. CIRCU has created a visual illusion of the skies. This round rug faithfully imitates white cumulus clouds floating on a deep blue sky and a reflection of the sun that is hidden from the scene. This realistic depiction tricks the eye and can inspire various games, from cloud watching and imagining which shapes they resemble to dreaming of flying among the clouds. The Griffin Rug by Bloomingville is a simple but very cute rug in the form of a single grayish-white cloud with closed eyelids. It looks great next to a bed or used as a play spot in a bigger space.

GRIFFIN RUG, BLOOMINGVILLE MINI

A TO Z WASHABLE RUG, LORENA CANALS

Decorating a rug with the ABCs seems like a perfect way to help children memorize each letter's shape and understand the connections between all of the symbols. Designers have created truly diverse compositions using the alphabet. Lorena Canals' design is based on a round form, and places A to Z around the edges to encourage movement. The light and soft rug is made of cotton and, due to its convenient size, is washable in a conventional washing machine.

SHAPED RAINBOW HOOK RUG, AMPERSAND DESIGN STUDIO AND PEKING HANDICRAFT, 2020

Possibly the most inspiring and visually stimulating theme is a rainbow. What can be more fun than walking or playing on one? Ampersand Design Studio draws from this colorful phenomenon to brighten children's rooms and does it in numerous inventive ways. Based on a simple curved form, the Shaped Rainbow Hook Rug is a vibrant composition of perfectly juxtaposed hues. It can be a lively addition to the bedside, softening each morning's first footsteps. The designers also demonstrate a creative take on the rainbow by decomposing it into inventively arranged elements, such as in the Roller Rink Rug.

ROLLER RINK RUG,
AMPERSAND DESIGN STUDIO, 2015
THE LAND OF NOD

#BEANBAGS & POUFS

Children adore all kinds of beanbags and poufs, not only because they are extremely comfortable to sit or lie on, but also because they are perfect for climbing and acrobatics. Soft and inventively shaped, they can be great sources of fun.

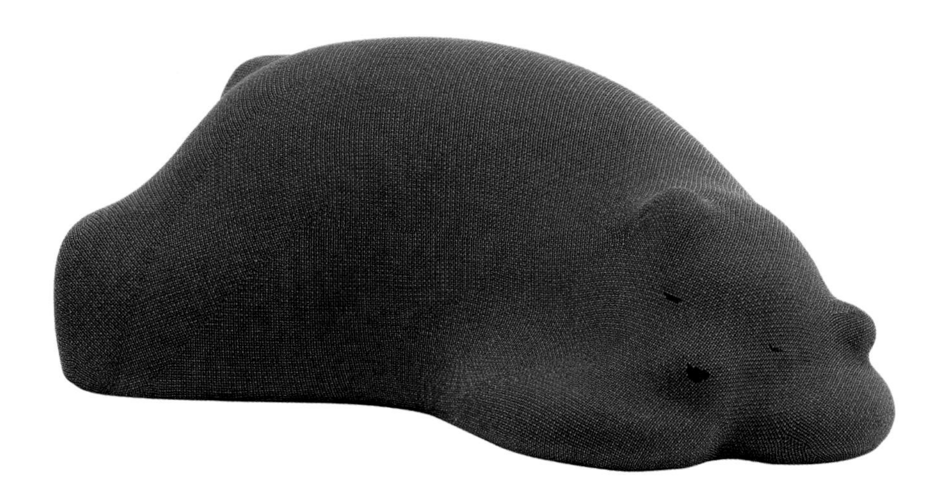

RESTING BEAR POUFS, FRONT, 2018 VITRA

"Numerous works by the creative duo Front are devoted to the systematic observation of sleeping or hibernating animals," explains the manufacturer of these adorable bears. The volumes, covered by knit fabric, rest tranquilly on the floor and invite the child to interact with them. One can hug them, climb over them, lie down and rest one's head on them, or use them as a backrest or a stool. The designers' goal was to create a sense of companionship and relaxation, which are both quite important for children.

RAINBOW VELVET POUF, PIA WEINBERG MAISON DEUX

The Rainbow Velvet Pouf looks like a piece of cake. Upholstered with velvet in three calm hues, it is very decorative though simple in form. It was envisioned as a multifunctional piece of furnishing. It can be used as a seat for children or an extension of a sofa, as the designer Pia Weinberg suggests. Pleasant and soft to touch, the minimalistic pouf encourages interaction. Smaller children can easily treat it as a mini slide.

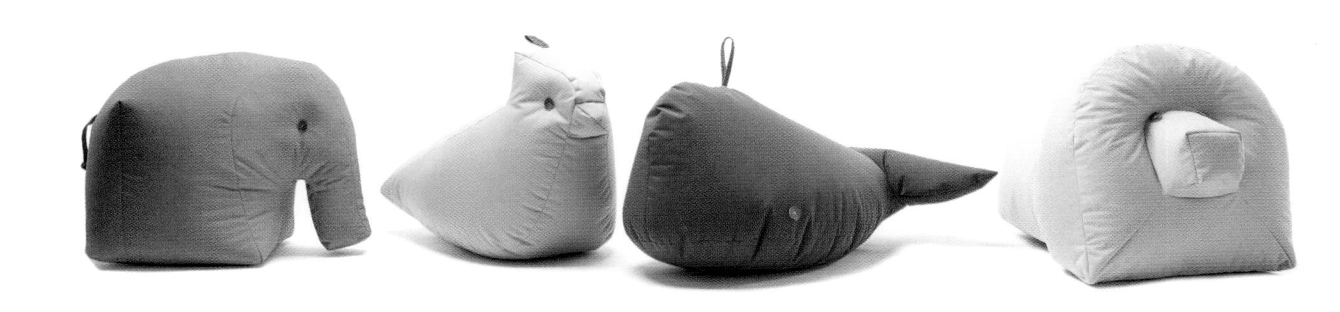

HAPPY ZOO COLLECTION, SITTING BULL

Thanks to this amazing collection, it is possible to recreate a zoo in one's room. "Happy Zoo" is a unique collection of animals to hug, sit on, and play with, which includes: Ben the whale, Carl the elephant, Fine the bird, Nora the lioness, and Lotte the horse. Made of robust material they are soft enough for the body, but at the same time they retain their imaginative form and remain stable on the floor, even when not in use. The soft colors definitely add to their appeal and make these beanbags even cuter.

ESSAOUIRA BEANBAG, NOBODINOZ

Beanbags also come in XL sizes, like the Essaouira series by the Spanish brand Nobodinoz. A child, or even a teenager, could easily stretch out on it comfortably and lean back on the triangular backrest. Despite its large dimensions, the beanbag is light to move around. With additional pillows, it can be the softest throne on the planet. Made of eco-friendly fabric and available in numerous patterns (they can be paired with other products of the same manufacturer), the covers are easy to remove for cleaning.

LIVING TOWER POUF, VERNER PANTON, 1969 VITRA

This iconic design by Verner Panton dates back to 1969 and is still popular today. The sensually shaped Living Tower is a sculpture-like seating system. The organic forms create niches for sitting on four different levels. The softness of the volume and its curved lines are highly inviting. It offers a relaxation area that is unusual, plus a socializing space that can be utilized by several people at once. The exact dimensions are 6′9″ x 6′9.5″ x 2′1″ (206 x 207 x 63 cm.) The stable frame of beech plywood ensures that the massive construction remains stable.

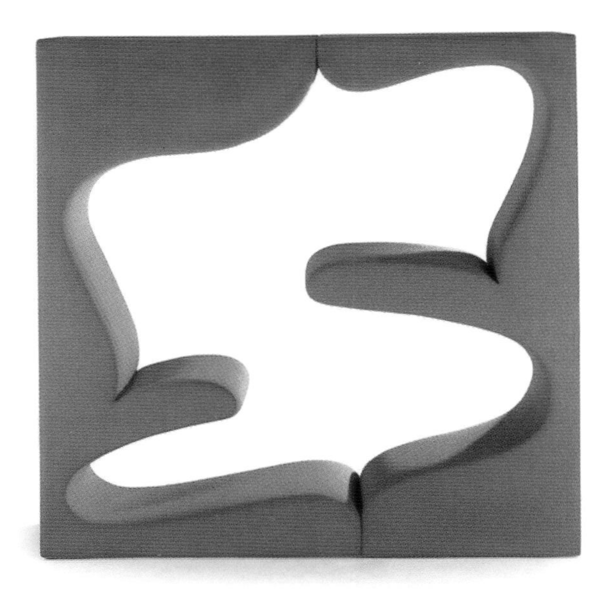

ROMANIAN BEARS
WALLPAPER,
ANNA STEAD
LILIPINSO

#WALLPAPER

The surfaces of the walls are an important decorative element. Wallpaper can be playful and can create a truly magical atmosphere, especially today, when a large selection of patterns and motifs makes the decision easy. We have selected a handful of examples from the leading manufacturers.

KOALA WALLPAPER, FERM LIVING

Animals are an obvious choice for wallpaper, and among them some animals are more popular with children than others. Bears and koalas appear to be in the lead. The designs created by Lilipinso and Ferm Living are based on single silhouettes of the animals, captured in various positions and repeated on a calm background. Despite numerous depictions, the pattern is not overloaded, but instead creates an elegant and quiet rhythm on the wall. By noticing the changing postures, children can train their observation skills.

DELLA WALLPAPER,
SANDBERG

SAFARI WALLPAPER, FERM LIVING

A wallpaper with a dense pattern featuring numerous elements in a chaotic composition encourages visual immersion. Forms are important here in addition to vivid colors. The result is a wall that is vibrant and alive, especially when saturated hues have been used. There are many themes suitable for this style, from sea creatures to exotic animals to forest life, which stimulate children's imagination and train their sense of observation. Motifs that cover the entire surface of the wall are visually strong and intense. Such a rich background needs to be balanced by simple furniture in a neutral chromatic palette. The nearly all black-and-white graphic pattern by the French brand Bien Fait is an interesting way to fill the surface in a similar manner, but without overloading it.

FOREST ANIMALS
WALLPAPER,
VERONIKA CARRENDER
LILIPINSO

WALLPAPERS
WITH ANIMALS,
BIEN FAIT

MULTI STEM WALLPAPER, ORLA KIELY / HARLEQUIN

The world of plants is always a great source of inspiration for designers. Organic patterns enhanced with color and repeating compositions are perfect for creating distinctive yet not dominating wallpapers. Padukka, available in three different color versions, focuses on the motif of a flower with a leafed stem against a monochromatic background. Subtle and fresh, it transforms large surfaces into a botanical garden. Multi Stem designed by Orla Kiely was inspired by the style of the 1960s. The characteristic hues and rhythmic arrangement have a resolutely vintage flair.

PADUKKA
WALLPAPER,
SCION

MOSAIC WALLPAPER, BIEN FAIT

Playing with colors and geometric shapes can result in splendid visual effects. The Mosaic Wallpaper will brighten up any space. The manufacturer describes the pattern as "triangles that unfold hypnotically into infinity," with "multiple facets that sparkle like a kaleidoscope of vivid and soft nuances." The large scale of the geometric forms as well as the visually delightful color contrasts make the wall shimmer. This wallpaper is a celebration of color and will speak to children's imagination.

ABRACADABRA JOUR PANEL, ISABELLE PARMENTIER ET MARTINE DUBREUCQ ISIDORE LEROY

For those who value more quiet solutions where the focus is on a single image that seems to be painted on the wall, a wallpaper panel will be a most satisfying choice. Captivating compositions, narrative motifs, artistic quality, and stunning colors characterize a wide range of designs. The Abracadabra Jour Panel shows the top of a massive tree with a night sky full of stars and planets in the background. Its fairy-tale, dreamlike composition encourages the mind to wonder.
The Wilton Panel is a poetic vision of a tropical scene with a lemur on a palm tree, a cat, a toucan, a flamingo, a bee, and cacti. With its subtle palette and watercolor-like style, it is very decorative.

3 2
WEEKS

WILTON PANEL,
SANDBERG

CLAIR-OBSCUR PANEL,
CAMILLE BAZIL AND ALICE RICARD
LITTLE CABARI

NAGAWIKA, CAMILLE BAZIL AND ALICE RICARD LITTLE CABARI

French manufacturer Little Cabari successfully combines charming illustrations with deep hues. Whether it is a forest with lush foliage or a scene from a Native American settlement on the Great Plains, their wallpaper panels create quite a special atmosphere in children's rooms.

GLOW IN THE DARK WALLPAPER, MINI ME COLLECTION EIJFFINGER

This wallpaper has a wow effect thanks to innovative technologies that make it glow at night. The dense composition of bright stars stands out from the dark background. "Between them sparks an infinitude of points reminiscent of stardust bringing us to distant planets," emphasizes the manufacturer, whose designs let children's imaginations run free and bring a spark of joy. It's a great idea that can replace a bedside lamp and make falling asleep magical.

#MIRRORS
Mirrors are useful accessories that are generally loved by children. Little ones observing their own reflections, especially as a form of play with their parents, can be highly educational and teach self-awareness, or can simply be fun (making faces in front of the mirror can result in a lot of laughter). Mirrors can generate interesting reflections or create the illusion that the room is bigger. Either way, they are magical objects that fascinate young design lovers with their mysterious superpowers.

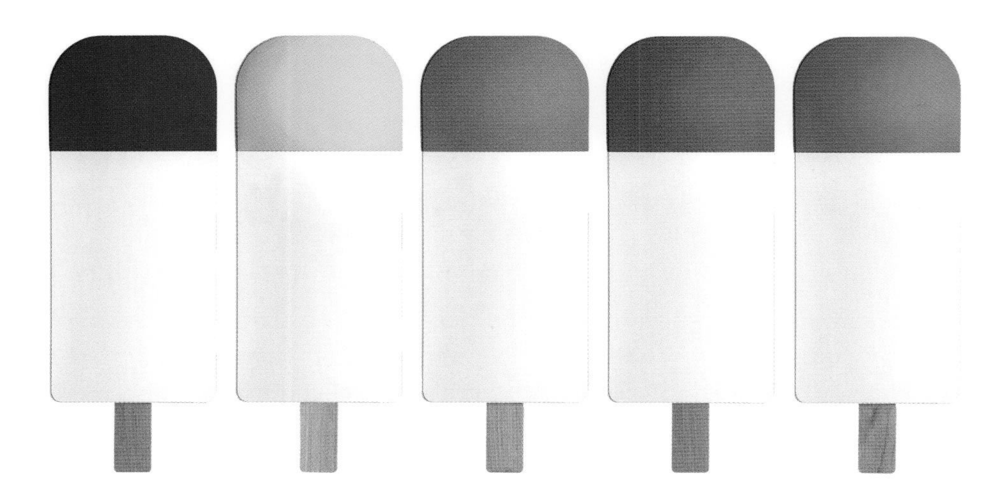

BALLOON AND ICE CREAM MIRRORS, NICOLE & TOR VITNER SERVÉ, 2014 EO

Both the Balloon and Ice Cream mirrors designed by Nicole & Tor Vitner Servé, the founders of EO, are decorative and playful. The Balloon, with its small wooden knot and leather string, comes in two sizes, and the slim Ice Cream is available in several colors. Inspired by children's favorite items, the mirrors will add humor to any space. With their imaginative shapes, the mirrors can be arranged in groups, they can fill even a small wall surface, and be placed on almost any level.

PANDA MIRROR, (WITH BEAR OPTION) A LITTLE LOVELY COMPANY

This lovely mirror is made of durable silver acrylic (Perspex) and comes with a hook. All one has to do is to find a good spot in the room, hang it and ... add the accompanying stickers. With two choices, the mirror can be transformed into a panda's face or a bear's. As the stickers are interchangeable and reusable, the fun can continue. And by choosing not to use the stickers, children can become bears by filling the contour with their own reflection.

#LAMPS

Lighting in children's rooms is essential. Whether a lamp hanging from the ceiling or one standing by the bedside, they should illuminate the space pleasingly and effectively. Designers have used countless innovative shapes and materials to turn this practical object into an artistic tool to shed light through the disquieting darkness.

FAVOURITE THINGS, CHEN KARLSSON ENO STUDIO

"Follow your inspiration and decorate this lamp with your favorite things!" encourage the designers, and they offer a lamp with a glass container below the bulb. Through a round hole in the container, one can put on display small toys, flowers, or any other small decorative objects. The object then will be delicately lit from above by the light bulb. Depending on what is placed in the transparent section, a magical play of reflections can be created in the room. The lamp designed by ENO Studio is available in five different colors.

A
F
K
O P
T
U
X

AIR BALLOON LAMP, CAM CAM COPENHAGEN

The ceiling as sky can bring many inspirational references that challenge a child's imagination. A hot air balloon is one of them. Scandinavian brand Cam Cam created a simple yet joyful design. The characteristically shaped lamp shade is made of cotton and diffuses a warm light. The lovely little basket underneath is made of bamboo to complete the light structure. Suspended from the ceiling, it creates the impression that it will rise through the roof.

CLOUD LAMP
CIRCU

Clouds typically hide the best source of light, but that hasn't stopped designers from using their forms as lamp structures. The hi-tech model by CIRCU includes light and sound systems that are controlled by a mobile app or a remote. Just as it is possible to select music, the light can also be easily adjusted for various colors, intensity, or even lighting effects, which will let the imagination run wild.

WAVE LAMP, ORIGAMI COLLECTION, KENNETH AND NELLIANNA STUDIO SNOWPUPPE

The designers of Studio Snowpuppe enjoy creating objects from paper and wood, of which the Wave Lamp is one of the best examples. Inspired by walks on the beach, it is made of masterly folded and overlapping sheets in one of five pastel colors. "While watching the waves at sea we realized we wanted to design a lamp that is able to recreate the feeling of the ocean's movement," explain Kenneth and Nellianna. Its sculptural shape offers a pleasing effect whether the lamp is on or off.

CAT LAMP AND DOG LAMP, GET OUT COLLECTION
CLOTILDE & JULIEN
ENO STUDIO

Zoomorphic lamps are whimsical and can bring a lot of fun into a space — this cat and dog duo is a good example. Made of MDF and available in six different colors, they can be used individually or paired to create a stronger effect. The 3D puzzle-like structure is completed with a massive bulb for the face and a visible red electric cord. The lamps are big enough to be placed directly on the floor. As they are light, they can easily be moved around.

PET LIGHT COLLECTION, MARCEL WANDERS, 2018 MOOOI

Another option for a lighting pet is Marcel Wanders' collection of lamps for Moooi. The sweet Uhuh, Purr, and Noot Noot (owl, rabbit, and penguin) are delightful with their rounded volumes and playful details. "Their frosted glass bodies, decorated with touches of gold, emit a sunny, heart-warming light glow," remarks the manufacturer. For each distinctive model, the designer selected elements characteristic of the animal, and enhanced them with gold.

MICKEY MOUSE© LAMP, FERMOB

Whether on a desk or a bedside table, this humorous lamp will bring a smile to anyone's face. Referring to the world-famous mouse, it consists of a round lamp model on a small base with two aluminum ears fixed to the top. Its simple form hides advanced technologies, however, as both the temperature and light intensity can be adjusted. The lamp is rechargeable via USB and can run from 7 to 25 hours. It can be also used outdoors.

OLO LAMP, JEAN-BAPTISTE FASTREZ MOUSTACHE

This ingenious lamp designed by Jean-Baptiste Fastrez can be positioned in three different ways – horizontally, vertically, or at 45-degrees. These useful options and the fact that the 2 LED bulbs create a spotlight effect, make it perfect for use in any location in the room. An original reference to binoculars, a super-8 camera, or an old flashlight, the compact volume is a fancy accessory that appeals to the imagination of small explorers. Interestingly, the lamp is ceramic, with colors enhanced by intense hues.

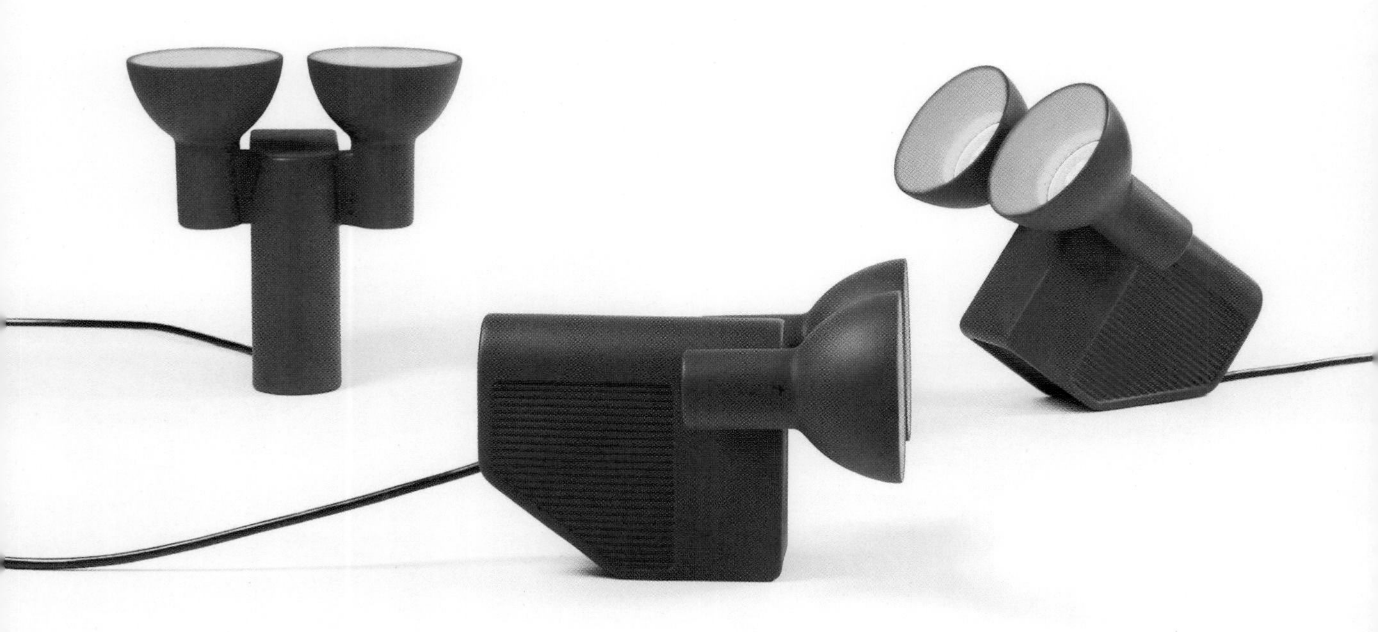

#MOBILES

Mobiles comfort toddlers by giving them the illusion of a presence above their heads. They also play an important role in the perception of shapes and colors from an early age.

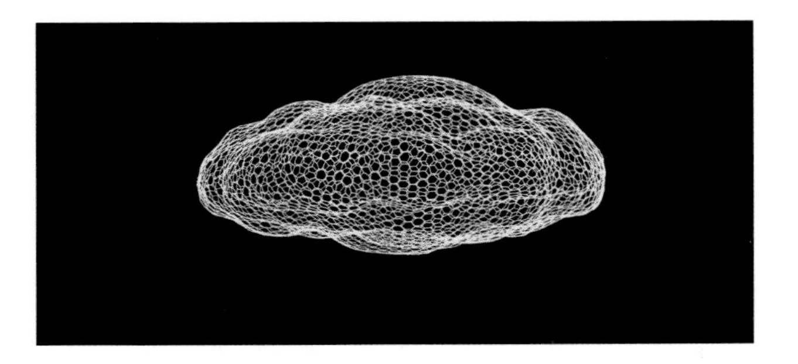

BIRD AND CLOUD MOBILES, BENEDETTA MORI UBALDINI, 2012 MAGIS ME TOO

Benedetta Mori Ubaldini designed a series of hanging sculptures of clouds and birds. The artist uses wire mesh, a simple and common material which usually remains hidden, to form an outer shell and leaves the objects transparent. Suspended in the air, quite literally on barely visible threads, they float and play with both light and the movement of the air. Both objects become subtle and sophisticated elements for an interior, introducing a poetic atmosphere reminiscent of a surrealist painting.

EXPRESSION MOBILE,
TINOU LE JOLY SENOVILLE
LITTLE BIG ROOM BY DJECO

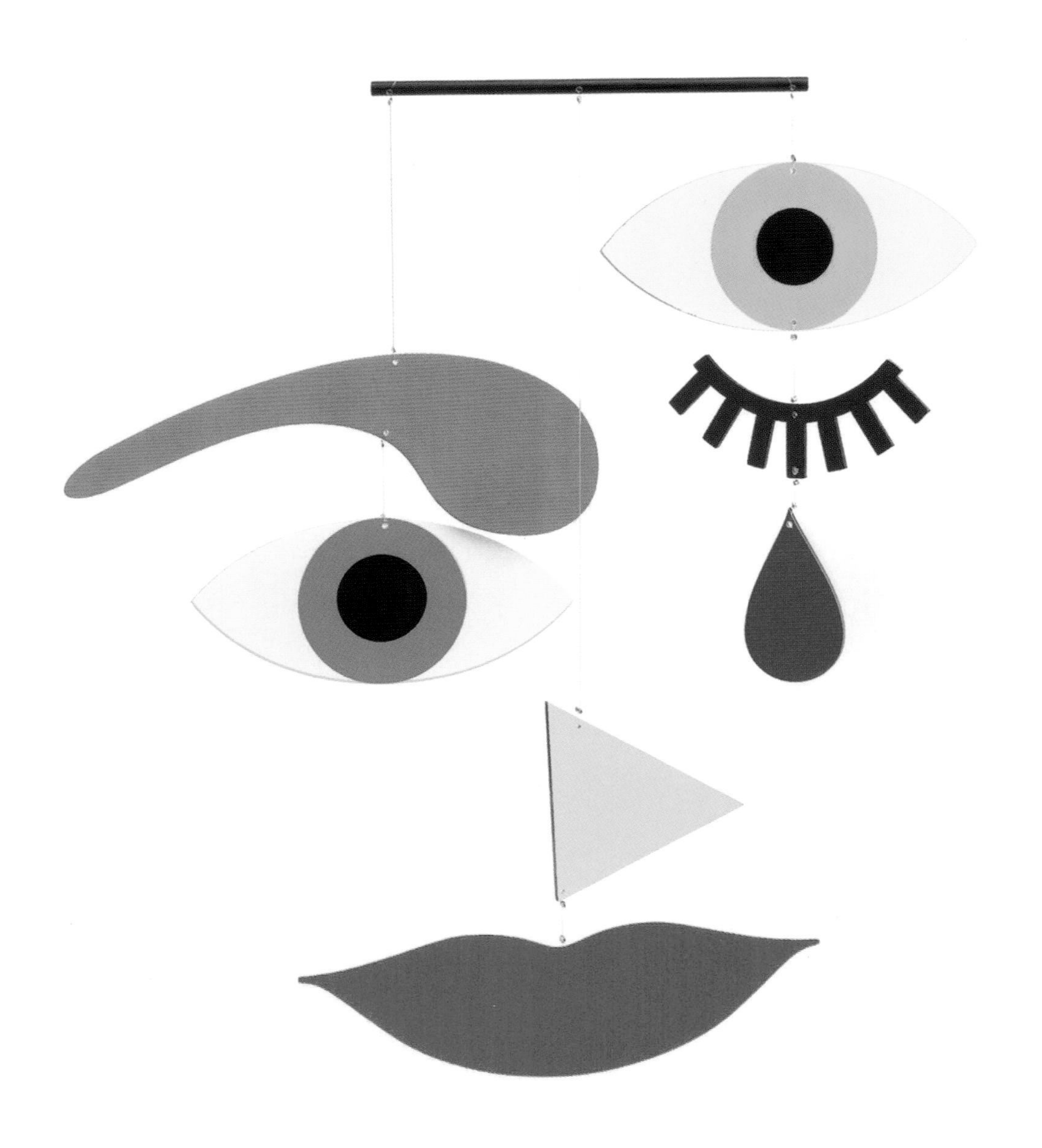

The keys to a perfect mobile for children, no matter what their age, are captivating shapes in dynamic interactions and vivid colors. Interacting with puffs of wind and often with the rays of the sun or artificial light, these elements create a most fascinating play of shadows on the walls. Many of them show artistic inspirations. Tinou Le Joly Senoville designed the Expression Mobile for the French toy brand Djeco. The scattered parts of a face seem to reflect various emotions and look as if they were elements from a cubist or surrealist painting. The Bauhaus Mobile was designed by Flensted Mobiles, a Danish company that specializes in mobile creations. Designed for the Bauhaus Museum in Weimar, it is built of geometric forms and relates to the characteristic Bauhaus palette of yellow, red, and blue.

BAUHAUS MOBILE,
OLE FLENSTED
FLENSTED MOBILES

#CLOCKS

Happy people don't count time, but it is always good to be able to keep track of it. Traditional wall clocks don't have to be boring, which is clearly demonstrated by the world's leading designers.

ZOO TIMERS,
GEORGE NELSON, 1965
VITRA

The Zoo Timers, by American designer George Nelson, are some of the best examples. Learning to tell the time is an enjoyable lesson with these amusing creations from 1965. Whether it's Fernando the Fish, Omar the Owl, or Elihu the Elephant, these playful shapes bestow the animals with personalities, but are simple yet very decorative. While distinctive, the numbers are easy to read, with each model using great color combinations that enhance the forms and readability.

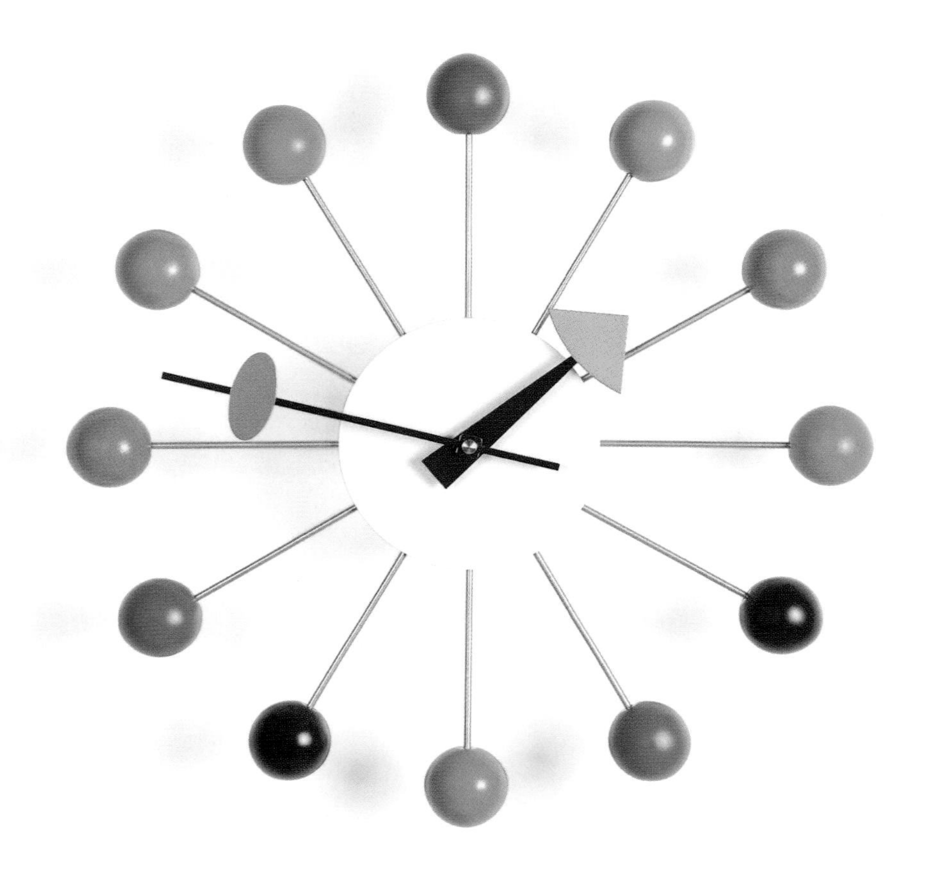

WALL CLOCKS – BALL CLOCK, GEORGE NELSON, 1948/1960 VITRA

Back in 1947 Nelson was commissioned to envision a collection of clocks and came up with 14 designs, one of which is the Ball Clock. As in the rest of the series, the clock doesn't use numbers. This was driven by his observation that people read the time by discerning the relative position of the hands. The clock's decorative quality comes from the fact that more and more people owned wristwatches, thus leaving wall clocks to be an element of décor. In this case the colorful balls and regular geometric structure do the trick.

FACE 2-6-10, AC/AL, 2019 EO

EO's design shows how minimalistic interventions can create an expressive object. The designers placed only three dots at strategic places (11, 2, and 6 o'clock); thus the hands of the clock become a sort of nose, creating faces with certain expressions. The clock demonstrates a simple but inventive way of touching upon the subject of emotions. The use of ABS plastic with a rubber finish and the pleasing palette of colors add to its soft and gentle look.

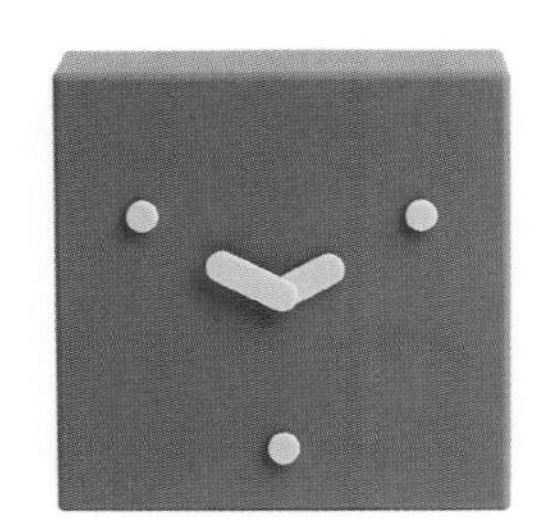

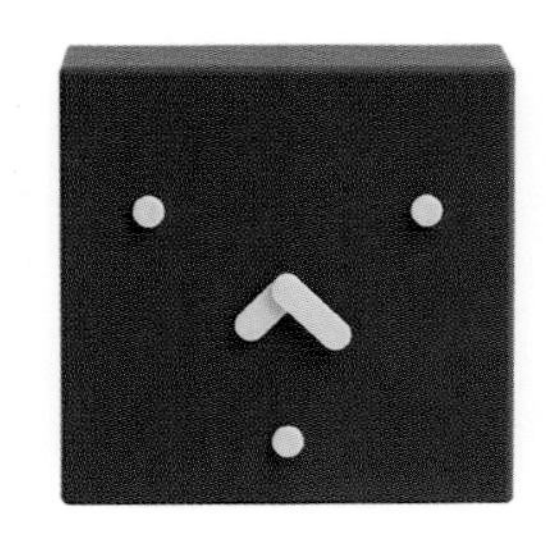

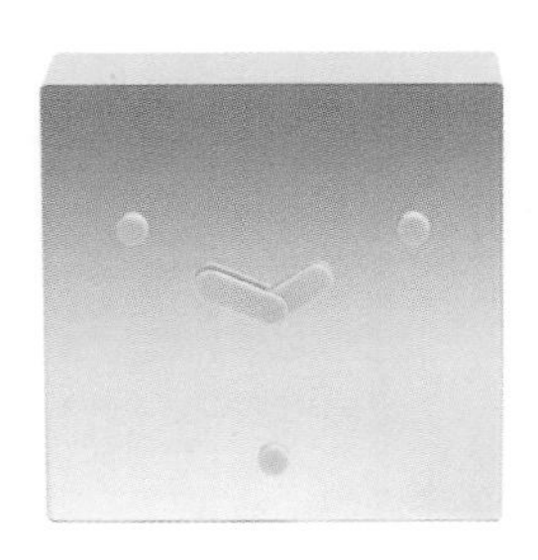

#COATRACKS & HOOKS

One of the biggest challenges in a child's room is maintaining order. In addition to a good system of boxes for usefully storing smaller items, there is also a need for a kind of hanger, whether a coat stand or wall hooks.

PARADISE TREE COAT STAND, OIVA TOIKKA, 2009 MAGIS ME TOO

The massive Paradise Tree coat stand is manufactured from polyethylene and can carry quite an array of things. The core of the designer's unconventional idea was to turn the pegs into cats, birds, and leaves. The combination is witty, especially in the version where each component on the tall tree trunk is in a different color. The shape speaks to the imagination, and it is fun to drape one's clothes and other stuff on a kind of tree, isn't it?

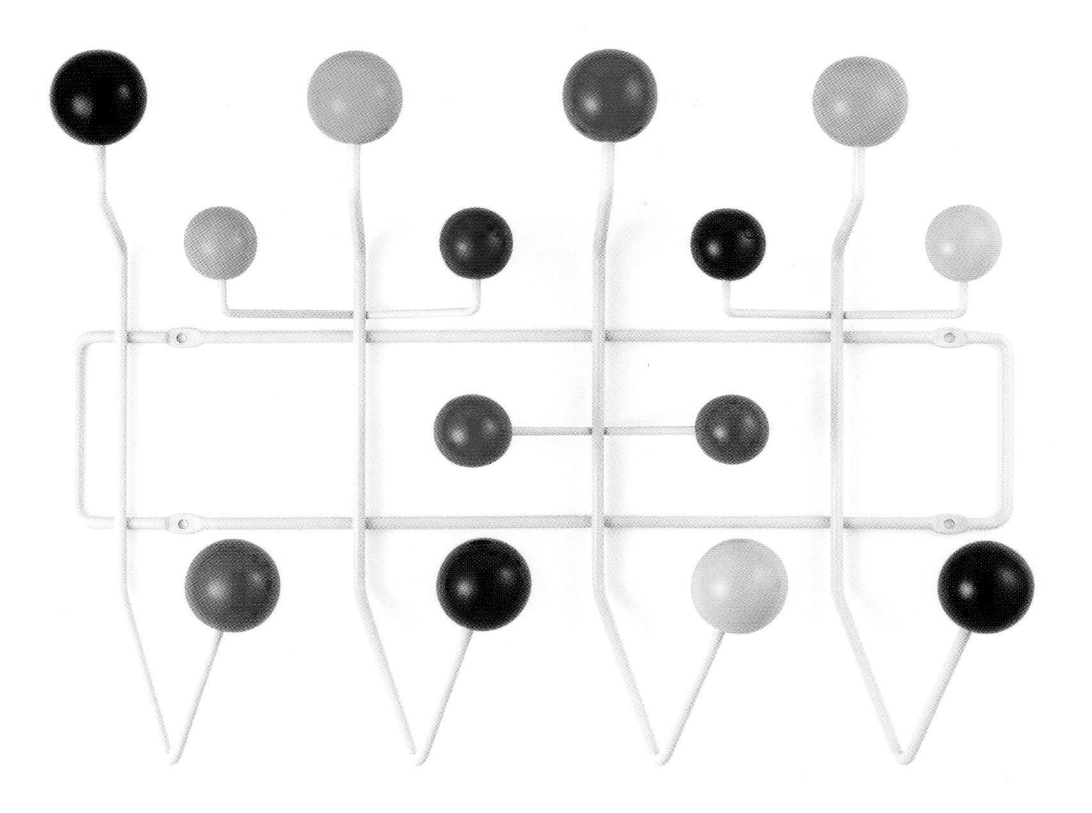

HANG IT ALL COATRACK, CHARLES ET RAY EAMES, 1953 VITRA / HERMAN MILLER

Designed by the famous designer duo Charles and Ray Eames in 1953, Hang it All is one of the fanciest coatracks in design history. Far from conventional, their combination of colorful wooden balls in two sizes looks playful and can accommodate many items. The rack is available in several color combinations, so it is easy to pair it with other decorative elements. Its simple but inventive shape is a lovely, stylish accent on any wall.

THE DOTS,
LARS TORNØE, 2007
MUUTO

Made of solid oak or ash wood, The Dots by the Danish brand Muuto can be painted in a range of vivid colors to create unusual visual accents on the wall. They are available in three different sizes, allowing for various arrangements. Attached to the wall, they look like buttons to push. Their smooth edges are safe and pleasant for little ones' hands to touch. Tornøe's dots are perfect for hanging clothes, hats, bags, or even hula hoops.

DROPIT HOOKS, ASSHOFF & BROGÅRD NORMANN COPENHAGEN

The designers Asshoff & Brogård also decided to use wood for their wall hooks but shaped them quite expressively in the form of drops. While a single drop looks interesting, arranging several in a rainy pattern creates a stunning visual effect. The drops come in black, white, coral, and natural wood hues so the combinations can be varied in many ways. The duo's creative goal, as they state, is to attract smiles and give a reason to raise eyebrows, which they have successfully achieved in their work for Normann Copenhagen.

ANIMAL HOOKS, FERM LIVING

The countless references to the world of animals are also evident in the hooks made for children, and designers have various takes on the subject. Ferm Living creates a series of ball hooks made of beech wood and painted by hand. Each basic shape is decorated with eyes, a nose, and a mouth to depict a panda, a rabbit, a dog, a sea lion, an owl, or a cat. The joyful expressions on their faces are quite captivating.

HOUSE WALL STORAGE, FERM LIVING

Speaking of hangers and organizing stuff, a wall tidy is a great way to keep the level of chaos under control. The design by Ferm Living is loosely based on the shape of a house. Made from cotton canvas, it can easily be hung on the wall thanks to a simple eyelet at the top and is flexible in terms of fitting items. Dorothee Becker's now iconic wall-mounted organizer is available in both a small and large version and is made of ABS plastic. It has containers in several shapes and sizes, creating a lovely geometric ensemble.

UTEN.SILO, DOROTHEE BECKER, 1969 VITRA

#TABLEWARE

In thinking about accessories, designers have not forgotten about tools for eating and drinking that add some fun to meals. Bright colors and fanciful shapes are the key to success. As Alessi, one of the leading manufacturers notes, "there is no age limit to a beautiful table."

ALESSINI – PROUST TABLEWARE
ALESSANDRO MENDINI, 2018
ALESSI

The legendary Italian designer Alessandro Mendini envisioned the Alessini – Proust collection to help children discover the use of tableware. The three pieces are decorated with multicolor dots similar in motif to Mendini's iconic Proust armchair. This inventive dotted style once again adds magic to the otherwise regular yet very practical ceramic shapes (such as a mug with two ears which not only looks a bit like a face, but also makes it easy for little hands to hold).

GIRO KID'S COLLECTION TABLEWARE AND CUTLERY, BEN VAN BERKEL / UNSTUDIO, 2020 ALESSI

"When you design a product for adults, you concentrate on its functionality and how to couple that with its materiality, aesthetic, and spatial qualities," muses Ben van Berkel of UNStudio. But, he explains, "something else happens when you design for children: different, more playful ideas start to rise to the surface, because you start to approach the design through the mind of a child." The designers' Giro collection includes colorful tableware and a cutlery set, which helps teach children how to use, hold, and balance each element correctly.

THE TWIST FAMILY CUTLERY SET, ALFREDO HÄBERLI, 2012 GEORG JENSEN

Designing a cutlery set is not an easy task. Stainless steel forks, knives, and even spoons are not really meant for children. To make them easy to use, the shape must be adjusted to children's hands, and it doesn't hurt to add a bit of humor to the design. Argentinian designer Alfredo Häberli not only uses funny shapes, which happen to be very helpful for grasping the cutlery and eating, but also adds hand-drawn faces on each element to make a family of four: mother fork, father knife, teaspoon daughter, and soup spoon son. Evoking positive emotions leads the users to feel happy at mealtimes. Animal Friends is a minimalistic set envisioned by Swedish designer Karin Mannerstål. The straight forms are finished with the faces of a monkey, a rabbit, a dog, and a cat, whose smiling heads gladly accompany children with each meal.

ANIMAL FRIENDS CUTLERY SET, KARIN MANNERSTÅL GENSE

EAT & LEARN SET, DESIGN LETTERS

The Danish brand Design Letters created a very simple, yet special, collection decorated with Arne Jacobsen's iconic typeface, designed in 1937. Driven by the idea of learning while eating, each element is covered with letters and numbers. The set comprises a breakfast bowl, a deep plate, and a dinner plate, all made of durable Tritan™, a medical-grade plastic safe for children, as well as a drinking glass with removable accessories including a sippy lid, a straw lid, and a handle for the youngest users. This timelessly elegant design turns each meal into an alphabet lesson, and is a feast for the eyes.

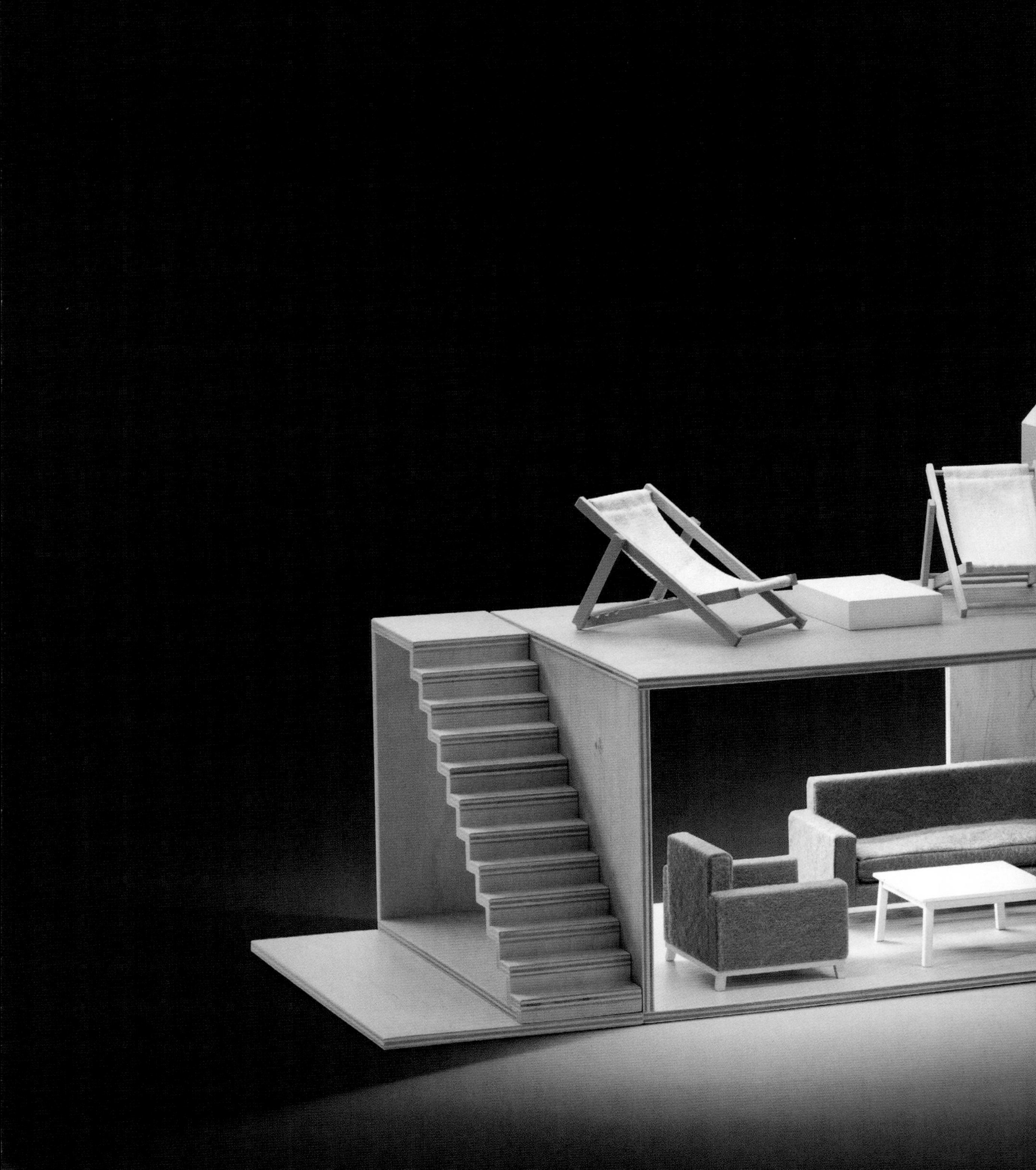

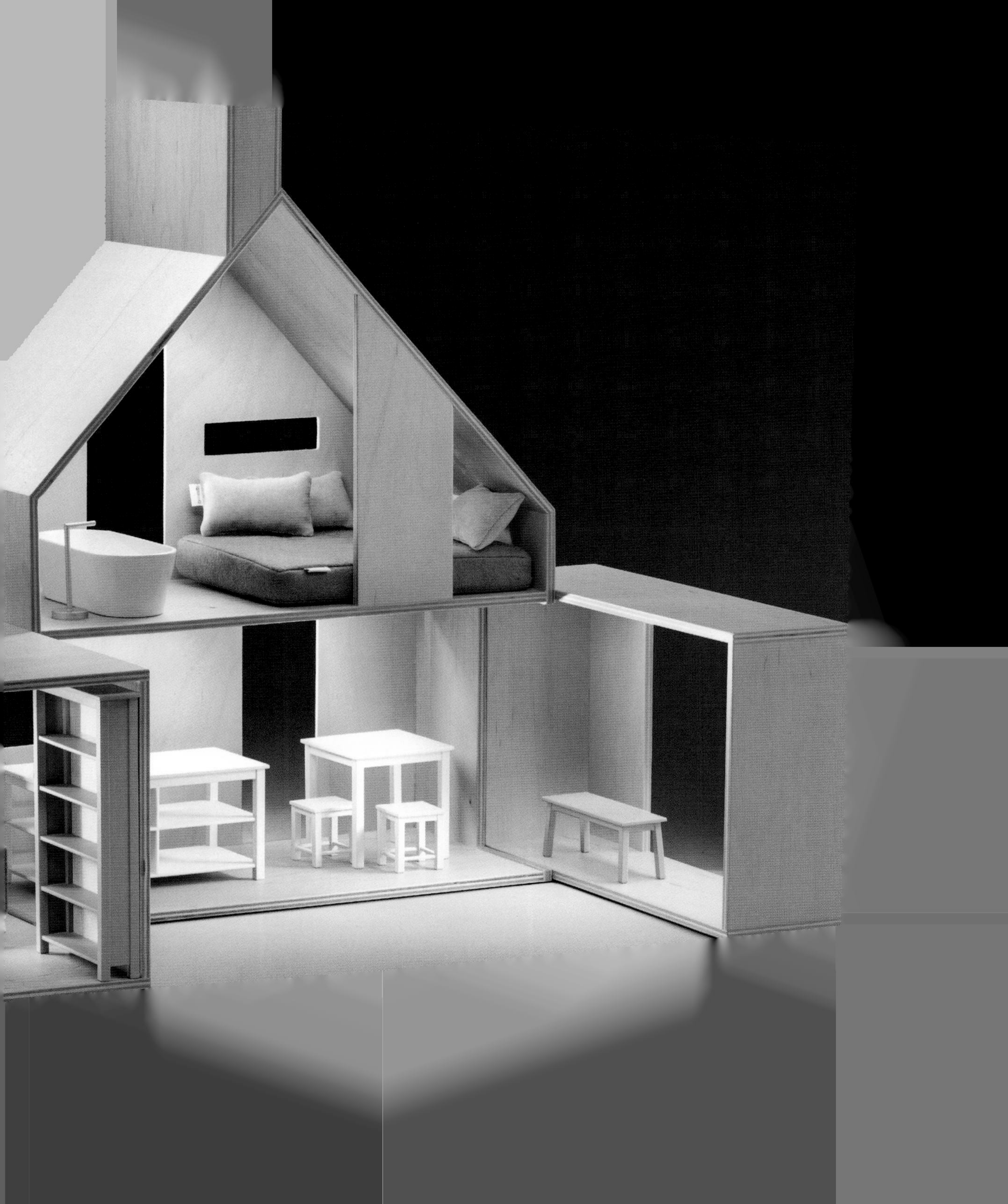

#ANIMALS

Children love visiting zoos, and they also adore animals at home. As parents may be less enthusiastic about this prospect, some designers offer great alternatives that will make everyone happy.

MY ZOO,
MARTÍ GUIXÉ, 2012
MAGIS ME TOO

Martí Guixé designed the My Zoo collection for Magis Me Too, with a giraffe, an elephant, a camel, and a whale. This set of gigantic animal toys that you put together is made of white cardboard, so the new zookeepers can color the creatures in any way they wish. The origami-like shapes make a big impact at this unusual scale. It is great fun not only to build them, but also to add one's stamp by decorating the result. Of course, after the assembly and decoration are completed, children can let their imaginations run wild.

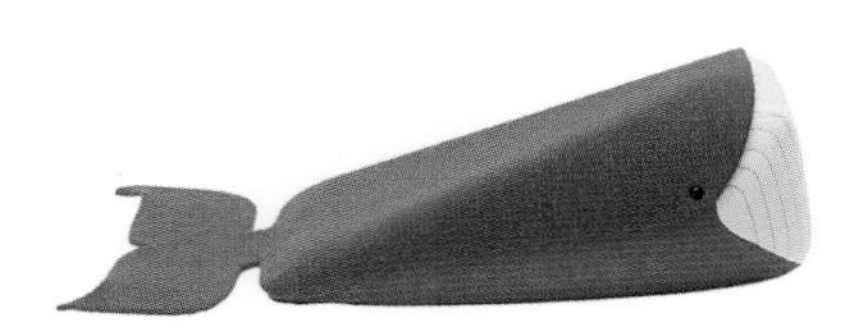

ZOO COLLECTION, IONNA VAUTRIN, 2016 EO

Another marvelous set is the Zoo Collection consisting of a panda, a toucan, and a whale by French designer Ionna Vautrin. Manufactured by EO, these cute, cuddly toys are based on regular-size 'teddy bears' but produced in a significantly oversized version. The little ones can interact by leaning or lying on them, hugging, or climbing. The limited palette of colors and sophisticated forms make it a very pleasing and original collection of toys. There is also an educational aspect, as these three animals represent the elements air, earth, and water.

ELEPHANT,
CHARLES AND RAY EAMES, 1945/2007
VITRA / HERMAN MILLER

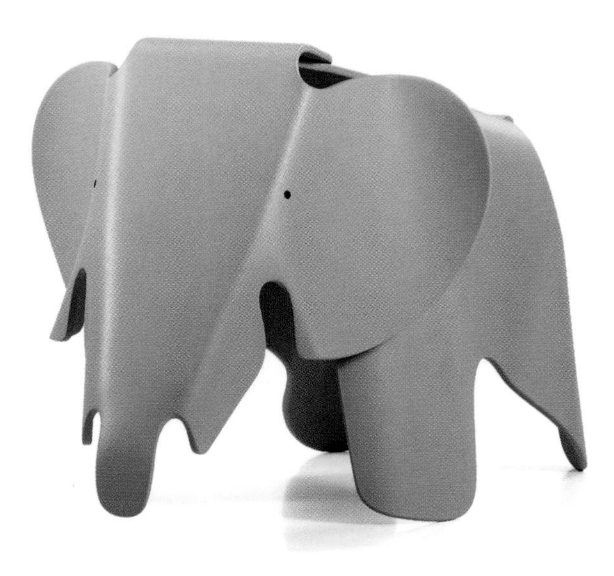

In the 1940s, the famous American designer duo developed a technique of plywood molding. The elephant was technically challenging, as its sculptural figure with prominent ears is made of two pieces that are tightly curved. The iconic Elephant toy by Charles and Ray Eames comes from 1945, but only went into production in 2007, and was initially produced by Vitra as a limited edition. Today the decorative animal is available both in wooden and plastic versions in a variety of colors.

PEACOCK,
TAKESHI SAWADA, 2013
EO

Drawing is one of children's favorite activities, and, theoretically, you don't need anything but a piece of paper and a set of crayons to create colorful visions fueled by your imagination. Nevertheless, this smart peacock can be very useful to young artists. The decorative wooden shape is the bird's body, adorned with numerous holes that can hold a wide range of colorful pencils to form the peacock's tail feathers. Created by Tokyo-based designer Takeshi Sawada for EO, the object is a lovely addition to any child's desk.

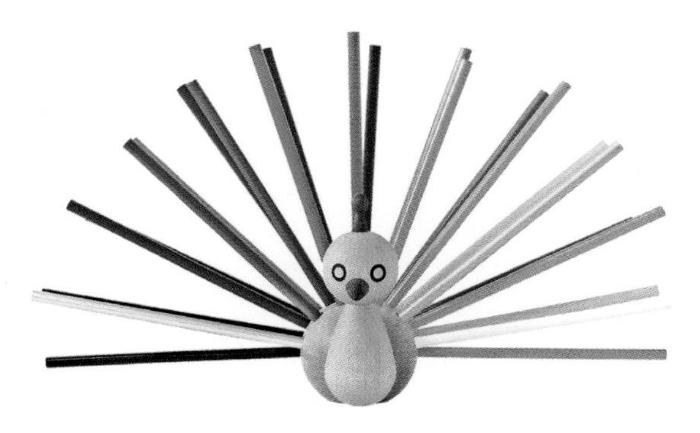

MONKEY, KAY BOJESEN, 1951 BRDR. KRÜGER

The Monkey's complex body consists of no less than 31 different parts. The legs and arms rotate while the monkey's hands and feet are shaped like hooks to allow it to hang and swing, just like its real-life counterpart. Manufactured by Brdr. Krüger, it is made of teak and limba hardwoods, which ensure the longevity of the toy. Kay Bojesen, who designed this iconic toy back in 1951 was known for his amazing skills in bringing wood to life with soul and humor.

Esben Gravlev takes us to the world of Goldilocks. The designer's little Baby bear, medium Mama bear, and big Papa bear are made of American walnut with accents from lighter wood marking the ears, the nose, and the feet. This natural and stylish small collection can be used as decoration or to re-enact the famous fable. For everyone who is fond of bears, Gravlev envisioned Teddy. "He is a tiny friend – one that will follow you through your life," states the manufacturer, adding humorously that he is "faithful, nurturing, and never complains."

WOODEN ANIMALS – BEAR FAMILY AND TEDDY,
ESBEN GRAVLEV
LUCIE KAAS

WOODEN BIRDS (TULA, BULA, PEPI)
KUTULU

This colorful collection of birds from Kutulu brings joy and invites interaction. Each model has a different name and color combination. To present but a few: Tula is a rocking bird and Bula is envisioned as an elegant swan. Both have a swivel head, while Pepi can sway gently. This is only a selection of the wooden toys by the brand, which are a pleasing mix of geometric forms, bright hues, and beech wood.

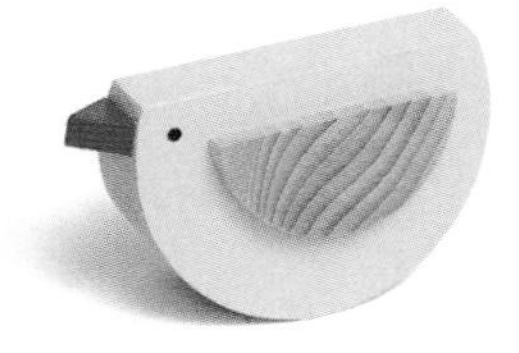

HAPPY BIRD, EERO AARNIO, 2015 MAGIS ME TOO

Animals play an important role in Eero Aarnio's practice. Nearly three decades ago, the renowned Finnish designer left Helsinki to be closer to nature. His proximity to the local wildlife and the possibility of observing numerous animal species inspired several of his designs. The idea of his Happy Bird figure, dating back to 2015, was fueled by the designer's habit of feeding the birds that don't migrate south for the winter. Grateful for being taken care of, they have become friends and happy birds.

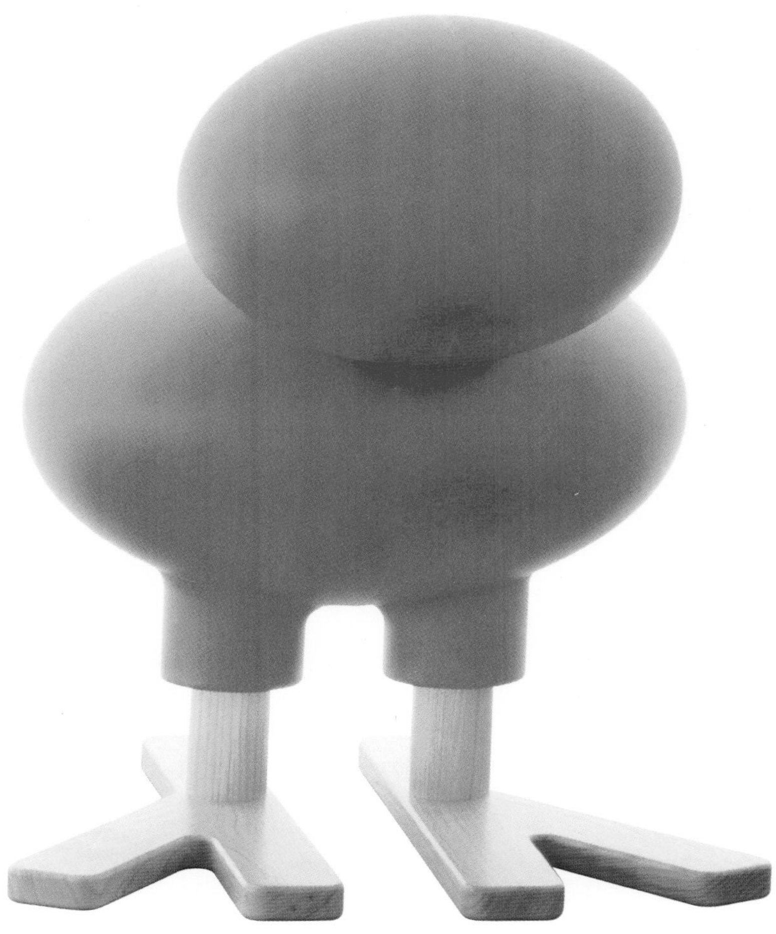

PINGY,
EERO AARNIO, 2011
MAGIS ME TOO

"As a young boy I made my first penguin out of papier-mâché, and when it was dry, I painted it black and white. For years this 7¾ inch (20 cm.) tall penguin lived on top of the cupboard in my childhood home," recounts Finnish designer Eero Aarnio. "Unfortunately, my apartment was destroyed in the 1940s during the bombing of Helsinki and the penguin was lost in the mayhem of war." Aarnio has since recreated the memorable toy. Pingy has a playful shape, mimicking the penguin's cute waddling movement.

PUPPY DOG, EERO AARNIO, 2005 MAGIS ME TOO

The Puppy Dog, designed in 2005, draws from the simplified way children see dogs. The rounded shapes of the head, the body with a tail, and the legs make it a lovely and funny pet, although a bit abstract. As it is made of polyethylene, it can be played with both indoors and outdoors. The Puppy Dog is available in four different sizes, so one can choose the height most appropriate to the child's age. It also comes in several colors, including a version with Dalmatian spots.

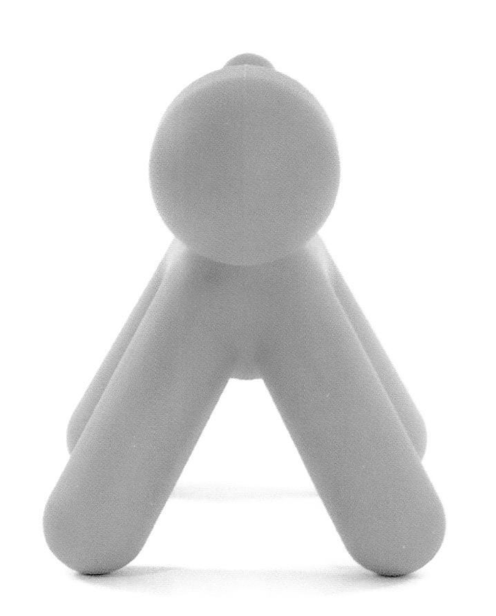

DORAFF,
BEN VAN BERKEL / UNSTUDIO, 2020
ALESSI

Described as a hybrid of a chair, a table, and a toy, the multifunctional Doraff combines the shape of a dog with a giraffe's characteristic long neck. The idea behind this inventive concept was to stimulate children's imagination. "Children can imagine they are riding a giraffe or playing with their dog, or they can easily flip over the lightweight figure to use the differently sized surfaces to play games, read, eat from, or simply climb on," explain the designers. Doraff is made of 100% recyclable thermoplastic resin.

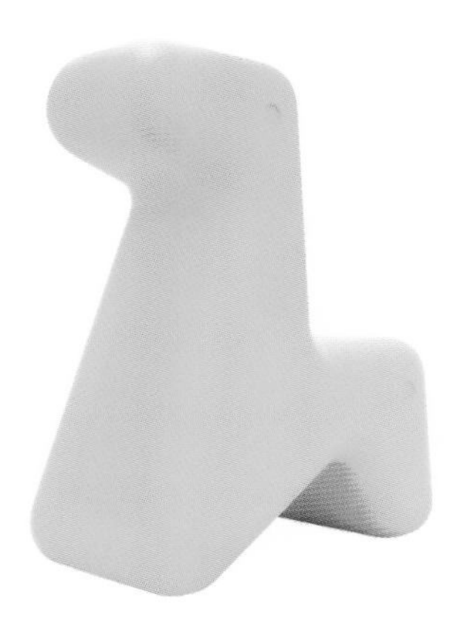

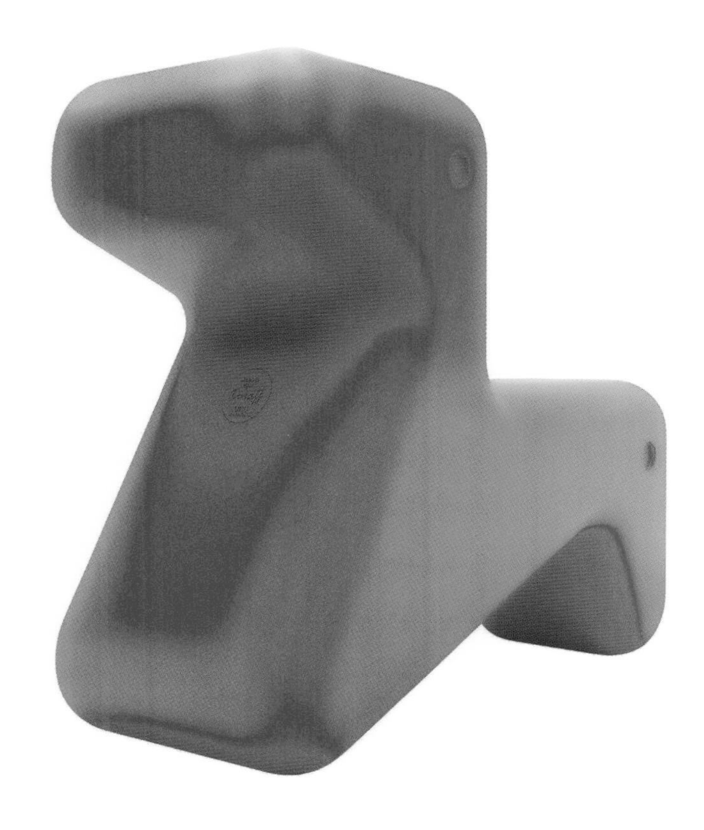

Hit the Road
nderstanding the World
1001 SONGS
WONDERPLANTS

HEROS

#DOLLS

It is impossible to imagine a childhood without dolls. As play partners and confidants of the youngest, they are simply indispensable.

KOKESHI DOLLS, BECKY KEMP SKETCH.INC FOR LUCIE KAAS

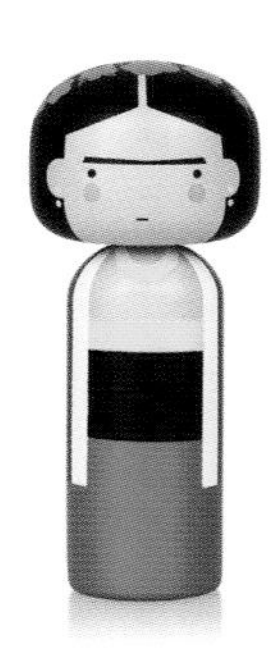

Kokeshi are Japanese dolls made of wood and characterized by their simple shape: a large head, without arms or legs. The Danish brand Lucie Kaas revisits this 150-year-old tradition to offer a stunning collection of contemporary incarnations. In collaboration with Becky Kemp, the brand created a collectible series including some of the greatest legends and icons in the fashion, art, music, and cultural world. The Kokeshi dolls are beautifully hand-painted and delight the eye with attractive colors.

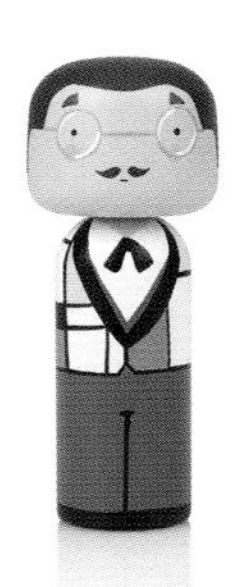

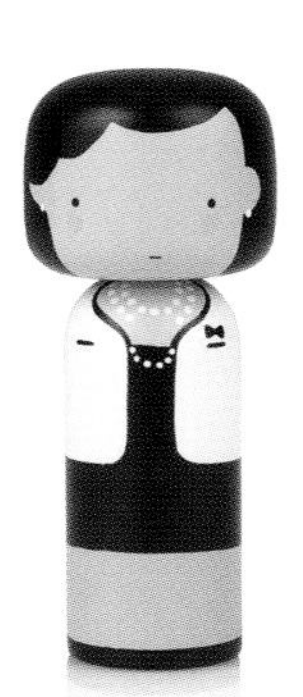

WOODEN DOLLS, ALEXANDER GIRARD, 1952 VITRA

Alexander Girard created a series of decorative wooden dolls for his own house in Santa Fe in 1952. He collected and had a fascination with the folk art of South America, Asia, and Eastern Europe. He brought home various textiles from his extensive travels and drew ideas from their patterns and textures. Girard was a master of playing with different color constellations and imaginative forms. These unusual forms are decorated with the most inventive patterns. Among the shapes, there is a very curious, angular black cat. It works well as a decoration or as a toy.

#ROCKING HORSES

One of the most iconic experiences of childhood is riding on a rocking horse. But forget about the traditional ones that resemble a horse. The form has been re-worked by many designers, so children today have a wide range of rocking horses, which may not even necessarily be shaped like horses...

H-HORSE, NENDO, 2016 KARTELL KIDS

H-horse, designed in 2016 by nendo for Kartell Kids, is an abstract rocking horse, reduced to three basic elements that mimic a horse's characteristic features. Its curving shape is executed in transparent methacrylate and it is available in four pastel colors. Light and modern, it is easy to maintain and takes up little space visually. Easy to sit on and grasp, H-horse may be minimalistic in form but it provides maximum rocking joy.

ROCINANTE, EERO AARNIO VONDOM

The revolutionary character of this creation by Eero Aarnio is that it not only brings joy to the little ones, but also brings a sentimental reminiscence of childhood to their parents. Rocinante comes in two sizes, as it is a rocking horse for adults and children. But this horse has other surprises. "Traditionally a rocking horse only rocks back and forth, but this horse has a base which also enables it to spin," points out the designer. Named after Don Quixote's horse, Rocinante is made of plastic and can be used outdoors.

FURIA, FRONT, 2016 GEBRÜDER THONET VIENNA

This expansive and curvaceous structure made of bent beech wood offers a large seating surface. The horse's typical features are treated schematically and with a hint of humor – its muzzle is a curved tube, while its little ears come in leather, just like the seat. The Swedish duo Front designed Furia in line with Gebrüder Thonet Vienna's signature style that was inspired by the manufacturer's greatest icon – the classic rocking chair.

ROCKY,
MARC NEWSON, 2012
MAGIS ME TOO

Rocky, by Sydney-born and London-based designer Marc Newson, is a serious challenge for the rider. The horse's massive silhouette, according to the designer, should provide the experience of sitting without ever being still. Designed in 2012 for Magis Me Too, Rocky was loosely inspired by medieval jousting horses. Resembling an actual animal, it is a perfect choice for children who dream of having their own pony.

MOKUBA, O&M DESIGN, 2011 BRDR. KRÜGER

In Japanese a rocking horse is called a *mokuba*. This one was designed in 2011 by the Japanese-Danish duo O&M Design, and was manufactured in a limited edition of 200 copies by Brdr. Krüger. The idea was to fuse the traditions of Danish craftsmanship and Japanese design philosophy, which resulted in a playful shape and a cheerful toy. Made from beech wood (with the tail made from vegetable-tanned leather), Mokuba is a minimalist yet fancy horse to ride.

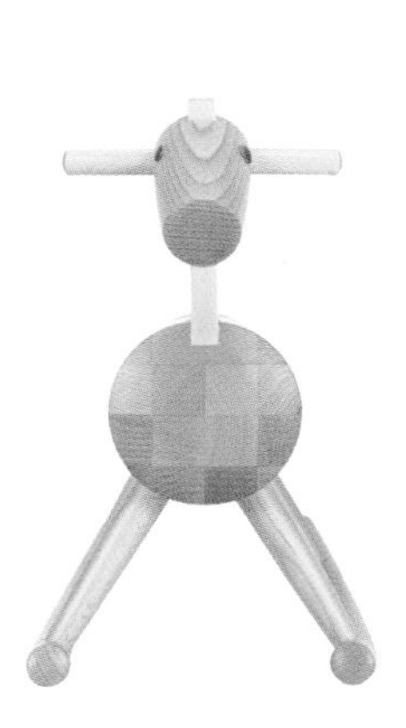

CLOUD, PIA WEINBERG MAISON DEUX

The designer and founder of the Maison Deux brand, Pia Weinberg, was wondering: "who said a rocking horse has to be an actual horse?" So she successfully created one in the form of a cloud. Rocking on a cloud? Why not? It takes the experience to another level, and children can feel as if they were suspended high in the sky. This poetic concept is executed in natural and durable materials. The frame is made of oak and the cloud has wool upholstery.

DODO,
OIVA TOIKKA, 2009
MAGIS ME TOO

If a cloud can replace a horse, a fancy Dodo will also make a great rocking ... bird. Created by Finnish designer Oiva Toikka, Dodo resembles the designer's glass sculptures, which are characterized by their defined shapes. Made of plastic, it is also suitable for outdoor games. The lack of handles allows more direct interaction with the figure. Children can simply lie on the Dodo, and let the bird rock them gently.

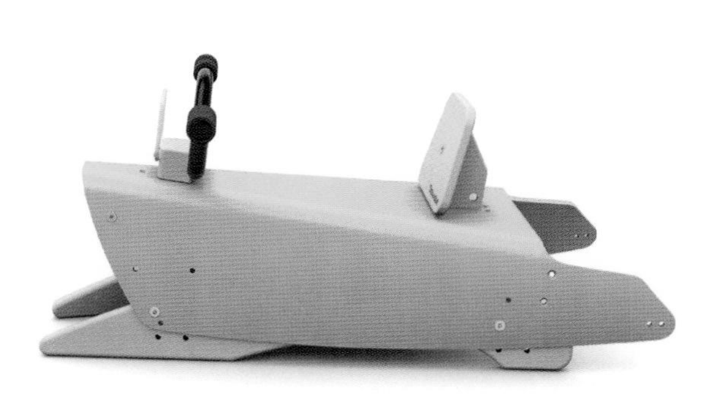

ROCKING MOTORBIKE, LAURENT LAMBALLAIS AND JEAN-MARC GOMEZ CHOU DU VOLANT

The rocking motorbike by French label Chou du Volant can be also used as a seat – the triangular structure in natural beech is reversible and can be transformed into a car or an airplane, depending on children's age and preferences. It also features a black steel handlebar with foam grips, flat footrests, and a tiny transparent windscreen. Designed to teach coordination and balance, it can be used by toddlers starting at age one.

#DOLLHOUSES, TEPEES & TENTS

Children adore recreating scenes from grown-up life, and re-enacting house scenes with their dolls, wooden toys, or animal figurines. Designers have envisioned ever more thrilling forms for dollhouses to make this happen.

MINI FUNKIS DOLLHOUSE,
FERM LIVING

FUNKIS DOLLHOUSE, FERM LIVING

This basic construction made from natural plywood consists of a terrace and five rooms, each of which has a unique shape and different window scheme. Divided across two floors, the house offers an expansive and inspiring space for playful arrangements. Whether dolls or animal figurines inhabit this modernist style house, fun is guaranteed. The structure's neutral walls can be creatively adorned, and the rooms can be filled with miniature furniture. As an alternative, the dollhouse may serve as an unconventional shelf.

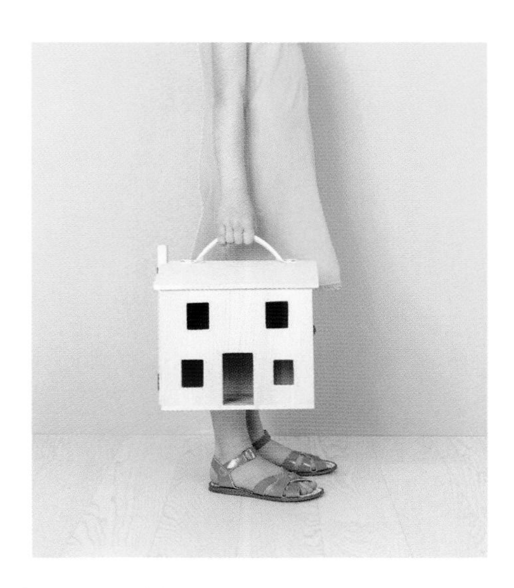

HOLDIE DOLLHOUSE, OLIVIA BROOKMAN OLLIE ELLA

This lovely, box-shaped dollhouse has a door, windows, and a handle on top. When it is opened, there are five spaces on two levels. The manufacturer, Ollie Ella, also offers a great selection of dolls and furniture that will gladly move into this lovely house. While it is made of pinewood (only the handle is made of vegan leather), the house is light and can be easily moved around even by young children.

MAISON RIVE GAUCHE
(LEFT BANK HOUSE),
W. SIRCH + C. BITZER, 2012
SIRCH

Sirch is a company specializing in wooden goods from packaging to furniture, and from sleds to toys. Their range includes very stylish dollhouses, which look like models from a contemporary architectural studio. Villa Sibis is a studio with a movable front and back that can also feature a roofed-in pool. Maison Rive Gauche is an expansive villa accessible from all four sides. The label also produces a sophisticated collection of furniture for their dollhouses.

VILLA SIBIS,
W. SIRCH + C. BITZER, 2004
SIRCH

MINI WOOD DOLLHOUSE, BOOMINI

This version is a downsized copy of boomini's WOOD model with a stunning and very realistic collection of furniture and accessories, which can be freely arranged. The 2-story cottage with a chimney and windows, stairs leading to the terrace, a living room (that can also become a garage), and a vestibule forms a multifunctional house that will inspire the imagination. All elements are made of natural materials, including high-quality plywood and wood, wool, and cotton. Each element is manufactured with an eye for detail, from cushions filled with anti-allergy inserts to professional upholstery foam mattress filling.

HARBOUR DOLLHOUSE, NOFRED

This portable dollhouse from Nofred was envisioned both as a toy for playing with, and as a space for storage. Crafted with sustainable materials, it consists of three levels covered with a pitched roof. While one of the façades shows a wall with a door opening, the opposite side is entirely open, thus allowing maximum access to the spaces. Additionally, there are openings on the sides and a skylight window to provide light. With a delightfully modern look, it is available in three colors – petroleum blue, pink, and gray.

MAISON EN BOIS (WOODEN HOUSE), THE CLOCK GABLE HOUSE, ALEXANDER OTTO WOODENPLAY

If dolls can have a wooden house, why not create one in a bigger size for children? WoodenPlay designed a fabulous cottage, large but made of light birch plywood, based on a screwless assembly system. The front looks like a classical Dutch façade, and the back has numerous simple openings, while one of the sides has a door and a window. A cozy place to read or cuddle with stuffed toys, it can easily transform into a shop. This house provides many great opportunities for creative play.

BALEAR HOME, NOBODINOZ

Let's look now at some interesting hybrids of houses and tents. Balear Home, given its large scale, is a nice hut that can be adjusted to any kind of game. The wooden structure is entirely covered with cotton fabric (with windows and door openings). All the sides can be rolled up with strings (only the roof remains fixed). Tinou is a one-piece structure, including the floor, covered with the most charming illustrations to create the perfect illusion of a tiny house surrounded by plants. The windows on both sides and the door can be opened. It is a fantastic toy for a lovely corner in the house as well as for sunny days in the garden. Adding small furniture or beanbags and poufs will turn these houses into real castles.

TINOU HOUSE, LITTLE BIG ROOM BY DJECO

TENT,
LAETITIA OLSAK AND CLOTILDE LE THÉO, 2016
MUM AND DAD FACTORY

A tent is a lighter version of a hideaway. Mum and Dad Factory presents a simple version consisting of a solid beech frame covered with white cotton. The light structure is easy to install. The Tent by Cyrillus has a more complex structure, reminiscent of a small hut. Its cotton cover creates a roof (with a window) and some walls. Both are perfect for playing or creating one's very own headquarters, best filled with the maximum number of cushions and rugs.

**TENT,
CYRILLUS**

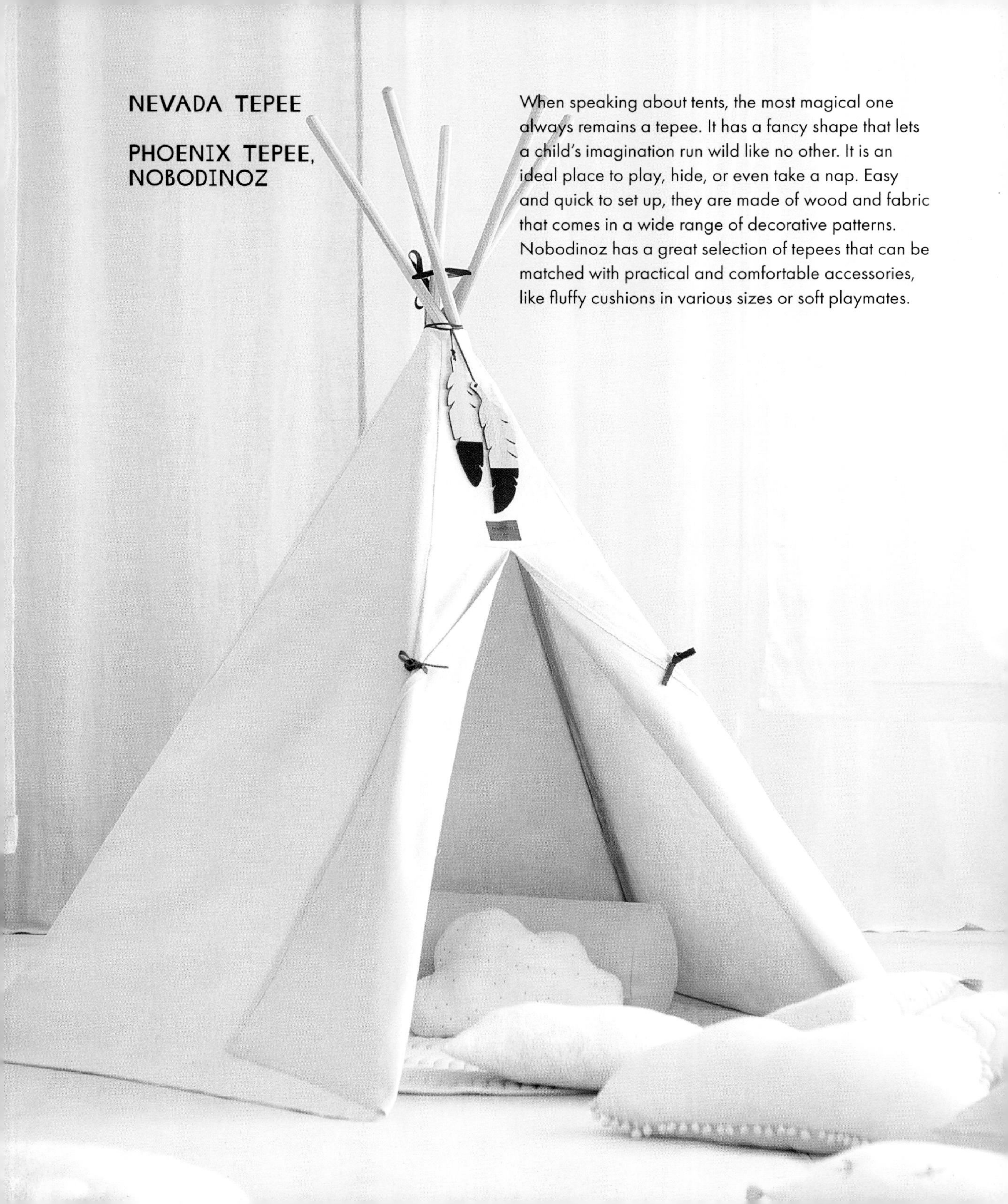

NEVADA TEPEE

PHOENIX TEPEE, NOBODINOZ

When speaking about tents, the most magical one always remains a tepee. It has a fancy shape that lets a child's imagination run wild like no other. It is an ideal place to play, hide, or even take a nap. Easy and quick to set up, they are made of wood and fabric that comes in a wide range of decorative patterns. Nobodinoz has a great selection of tepees that can be matched with practical and comfortable accessories, like fluffy cushions in various sizes or soft playmates.

VILLA JULIA,
JAVIER MARISCAL, 2009
MAGIS ME TOO

Playful houses can also be made of cardboard. The Villa Julia, with its distinctive cartoon flair, can be personalized with a set of lovely stickers or simply with drawings on the walls. "The most important thing is to have a house to their own scale, a private space made to their measure, where children can hide and play, sheltered by walls and a roof, where only children can be invited in, while no adults are allowed," explains Javier Mariscal, the designer of this ingenious house.

PLAYHOUSE MIFFY, MISTER TODY

Cardboard is eco-friendly and will never be boring. Playhouse Miffy is another great example of a cardboard house. Miffy, the world's most famous bunny, invites the children into a lovely little house for playtime fun. The structure, which is easy to assemble, is colored in children's favorite hues of vivid red, blue, and yellow. It also comes in a white version that lets the imagination run free for creative intervention through painting, drawing, or stickering.

NIDO,
JAVIER MARISCAL, 2005
MAGIS ME TOO

This original, bug-like organic shape, with openings at each end and whimsical eyes and legs, really sparks the imagination and invites interaction. Jumping into the belly of this funny creature feels like great fun. The rotationally molded polyethylene used for the structure is durable and easy to clean, plus it is also suitable for outdoor use. The green floor has a grass-like pattern, while the underside of the yellow roof has graffiti. A dream playhouse or hideaway, nest, or cave!

HOW TO DRAW ALMOST EVERYTHING
Wir zeichnen Tiere
11
10
9
8
7

KRICKEL-KRAKEL
RUDYARD KIPLING
JUNGLE BOOK
Where Is the
mutig, mutig

INDEX

PHOTO CREDITS

(l : left, r : right, t : top, b : bottom, m : middle)
Cover and pages 6-7: all objects are featured in the book, the photo credits can be found below.

366 CONCEPT: p. 16 © 366 Concept / photography, art direction & styling: Agata Górka
A LITTLE LOVELY COMPANY: pp. 166-167 © alittlelovelycompany.com
ALESSI: pp. 194, 195b, 211 © Alessi, p. 195t © Matteo Imbriani, pp. 212-213 © Inga Powilleit
ALINEA: p. 119-121, 128-129, 134r, 135 © Alinea
AMPM : pp. 76-77 © AMPM, Emmanuel Gallina
AMPERSAND DESIGN STUDIO: p. 140 © Ampersand Design Studio, Peking Handicraft, p. 141 © Ampersand Design Studio, The Land of Nod
ARTCANBREAKYOURHEART: pp. 50-51 © Sascha Grewe
ART FOR KIDS BY AFKLIVING: pp. 130-131, 134l © AFKliving
ARTEK: pp. 18-19 © Artek / photography: Mikko Ryhänen, p. 44 © Artek, pp. 18-19, 44 Courtesy of Alvar Aalto Foundation
BB ITALIA: pp. 14-15 © Courtesy of B&B Italia – www.bebitalia.com
BERMBACH HANDCRAFTED: pp. 70, 71 © Bermbach Handcrafted
BIEN FAIT: pp. 153, 156-157 © Bien Fait / photography: Cécile Figuette
BLOOMINGVILLE MINI: p. 136 © Bloomingville Mini
BONNESOEURS®: pp. 95-97 Bonnesoeurs®
BOOMINI: pp. 198-199, 229 © Boomini
BOQA: p. 36 © Boqa
BRDR. KRÜGER: pp. 73, 204, 220 © Brdr. Krüger
CAM CAM COPENHAGEN: pp. 170-171 © Cam Cam Copenhagen
CARL HANSEN & SØN: p. 54 © Carl Hansen & Søn
CASSINA: pp. 11, 42-43 © Cassina © VG Bild-Kunst, Bonn 2021
CHOU DU VOLANT: p. 223 © Chou Du Volant
CIRCU: pp. 98, 99, 136-137, 172-173 © Circu
CYRILLUS: p. 235 © Cyrillus
DESIGN LETTERS: p. 197 © Design Letters
ECOBIRDY: p. 62 © ecoBirdy / photography : Ulrika Nihlén
EIJFFINGER: p. 164 © Eijffinger
ENO STUDIO: pp. 168, 169, 176 © ENO Studio
EO: pp. 47, 55, 124, 165, 187, 203, 252 © EO, p. 201 © EO / photography: M Giesbrecht
FERM LIVING: pp. 58, 59, 149, 151, 192, 193, 224, 225t © Ferm Living
FERMOB: p. 37 © Fermob, p. 178 © Fermob / photography: Sebastien Erome, p. 255 © Fermob / photography: Jérôme Galland
FLENSTED MOBILES: p. 183 © Flensted Mobiles, Denmark – flensted-mobiles.com © VG Bild-Kunst, Bonn 2021
FOR CURLY: p. 111 © ForCurly
FRITZ HANSEN: p. 21 © Fritz Hansen
GEBRÜDER THONET VIENNA GmbH: p. 218 © Furia designed Front for Gebrüder Thonet Vienna GmbH (GTV)
GENSE: p. 196b © Gense
GEORG JENSEN: p. 196t © Georg Jensen
HAPPIEST BABY: p. 75 Courtesy of © fuseproject
HAY: pp. 5, 28 © Hay
IO KIDS DESIGN: pp. 90, 91 © IO Kids Design / photography: Karl Anderson, Stockholm
ISIDORE LEROY: p. 158-159 © Isidore Leroy
JUNGLE BY JUNGLE: p. 60 © Jungle by Jungle
KARTELL: pp. 22b, 100, 114, 216 © Kartell
KNOLL INC.: pp. 10 © Courtesy of Knoll, Inc. © VG Bild-Kunst, Bonn 2021, p. 12 © Courtesy of Knoll, Inc., p. 13, 52 © Courtesy of Knoll, Inc. / photography: Joshua McHugh
KUTIKAI: pp. 8-9, 64-65, 94 © Kutikai
KUTULU: p. 206t © Kutulu / photography : Michaela Sidorova, p. 206b © Kutulu
LAURETTE: pp. 61, 78, 87, 109 © Laurette / photography: Thomas Dhellemmes, styling: Juliette de Cadoudal, p. 86, 115 © Laurette / photography: David Bailleux / styling: Laure Bailleux
LEÇONS DE CHOSES: p. 101 © Leçons de choses / photography: Corine Schanté Angelé
LILIPINSO: pp. 148, 152 © LILIPINSO
LITTLE BIG ROOM BY DJECO: pp. 118, 182, 233 © Djeco
LITTLE CABARI: p. 127 © Little Cabari, p. 162, 163 © Little Cabari / architecture : Christine Guillaume, Studio Beaupassage
LORENA CANALS: pp. 125, 138, 139 © Lorena Canals
LUCIE KAAS: pp. 205, 214 © Lucie Kaas
MAGIS ME TOO: pp. 1, 24, 25, 26, 27, 30, 31, 32, 33, 35, 40, 41, 68, 88-89, 106-107, 108, 112, 113, 116b, 117, 180, 181, 188, 200, 207, 208-209, 210, 219, 222, 238, 239, 242, 243 Special thanks to © Magis Me Too, pp. 24-25, 32-33, 40, 108, 112-113, 116-117, 188, 222, 238-239, 242-243 © VG Bild-Kunst, Bonn 2021
MAISON DADA: p. 17 © @maisondada
MAISON DEUX: pp. 143, 221© designed by Pia Weinberg, brand : Maison Deux
MDF ITALIA: p. 29 © MDF Italia
MISTER TODY: pp. 240, 241© Mister Tody
MOOOI: p. 177 © Moooi
MOUSTACHE: pp. 48, 105, 179 © Moustache
MUM AND DAD FACTORY: pp. 104, 234 © Mum and Dad Factory
MUUTO: p. 190 © Muuto
NIKA ZUPANC: p. 74 © Nika Zupanc
NOBODINOZ: pp. 145, 232, 236, 237 © nobodinoz
NOFRED: p. 230 © Nofred
NORMANN COPENHAGEN: p. 191 © Normann Copenhagen
ŒUF NYC: p. 20 © Œuf Nyc
OLIVER FURNITURE: pp. 2, 53, 93 © oliverfurniture
OLLIE ELLA: p. 225b © Ollie Ella / photography: Penny Wincer, pp. 226-227 © Ollie Ella / photography: Patrick Stein
ORLA KIELY: p. 154 © Harlequin – Orla Kiely, Sanderson Design Group
PETITE FRITURE: p. 46 © Hanna Emelie Ernsting, Petite Friture
PILEPOIL: p. 126 © Pilepoil
PLANTOYS: p. 56 © PlanToys
PLYROOM: p. 92 © Plyroom / styling : Stefanie Ingram / photography : Martina Gemmola
RAFA-KIDS: pp. 83-85, 102-103 © Rafa-kids
ROCHE BOBOIS: pp. 63t © www.roche-bobois.com, p. 63b © Roche Bobois / photography: Michel Gibert www.gibson.com
SANDBERG: pp. 150, 122-123, 160-161 © Sandberg
SCION: pp. 132, 133, 155 © Scion Sanderson Design Group
SIRCH: p. 228 © Sirch / photography: Markus Dloughy
SITTING BULL: p. 144 © Sitting Bull
SMALL-DESIGN: pp. 66, 67, 110 © Small-Design
STOKKE®: pp. 79, 80, 81 © Stokke®
STUDIO SNOWPUPPE: pp. 174, 175 © Studio Snowpuppe
STUDIOS KALON: p. 82 © Courtesy of Kalon Studios
TECTA: p. 72 © Tecta / HGEsch
TOLIX®: p. 34tl © Tolix® / photography J. Mauloubier, pp. 34, 69, 116hm © Tolix®
VITRA: pp. 22h, 23, 146, 147 © Vitra / Courtesy of Verner Panton Design AG, www.verner-panton.com, pp. 45, 142, 184, 185, 186, 193, 244-245 © Vitra, p. 215 © Vitra / Courtesy of Girard Studio, pp. 189, 202 © Vitra / Hermann Miller. Likeness of the Hang-it-All and Elephant are used by permission of Eames Office LLC. All rights reserved.
VONDOM: pp. 38-39, 217 © Vondom
WE DO WOOD: p. 57 © We Do Wood
WOODENPLAY: p. 231 © Alexander Otto, woodenplay.eu
ZIETA STUDIO: p. 49 © Ploop Stool Mini (designed by Oskar Zieta) / photography: Marta Więcek. Courtesy of Zieta Studio

ACKNOWLEDGMENTS

This book would probably not have seen the light of day without the enthusiasm of Isabelle Dartois, éditions de La Martinière, who guided me brilliantly through this project. I would like to thank her once again for this. Thanks also to Allison Silver Adelman for her attentive proofreading.

I am very grateful to all the designers, manufacturers, and artisans who supported this book: it is a tribute to their unbridled creativity for the benefit of young people.

Thanks to all the parents of young children who encouraged me to persevere. I hope they will find, throughout these pages, ideal solutions for their little ones.

Finally, many thanks to my daughter Émilie, who will be celebrating her fifth birthday when the English edition of this book is published. Without her, I would not have had the idea to explore this fascinating subject.

First published in English in 2022 by Merrell Publishers,
London and New York

Merrell Publishers Limited
70 Cowcross Street
London EC1M 6EJ

merrellpublishers.com

First published as *Le Design pour les enfants* in 2021
by Éditions de La Martinière, Paris

A catalogue record for this book is available from the
Library of Congress.

British Library Cataloguing in Publication Data. A catalogue record for this book is available from the British Library.

ISBN 978-1-8589-4700-6

Produced by Merrell Publishers Limited
Copy-edited by Allison Silver Adelman

Printed and bound in China

AGATA TOROMANOFF is an art and design historian who has curated numerous contemporary art projects. She has written features for the art press and is the author of several books, including *Chairs by Architects* (2016), *Sofas: 340 Iconic Designs* (2018), and *Vases: 250 State-of-the-Art Designs* (2019).